JB JOSSEY-BASS™
A Wiley Brand

T0317730

Motivating Volunteers

109 Techniques to Maximize Volunteer
Involvement & Productivity

Scott C. Stevenson, Editor

WILEY

978-1-118-69057-4   ISBN

978-1-118-70417-2   ISBN (online)

Motivating Volunteers
109 Techniques to Maximize Volunteer Involvement & Productivity

Published by
Stevenson, Inc.

P.O. Box 4528 • Sioux City, Iowa • 51104
Phone 712.239.3010 • Fax 712.239.2166
www.stevensoninc.com

TABLE OF CONTENTS

TABLE OF CONTENTS

Motivating Volunteers: 109 Techniques to Maximize Volunteer Involvement & Productivity

SETTING GROUND RULES: GOALS, EXPECTATIONS & USEFUL TOOLS

Establishing clear performance and behavior guidelines sets the partnership between volunteer and nonprofit and up for success — just as failing to do so invites misunderstanding and difficulty. Lay the foundations for outstanding performance and achievement by making organizational expectations clear from day one.

Volunteer Guide Is Important for Successful Volunteering

Look for services within your community that promote volunteer opportunities, then take the steps needed to have your organization included in their offerings.

Persons seeking volunteer opportunities in the Denver, CO, area, can turn to Metro Volunteers (Denver, CO) — an organization dedicated to helping individuals, volunteers, corporate and community groups find volunteer opportunities. The organization's annual volunteer guide includes volunteer opportunity descriptions, age restrictions and contact information and allows volunteers in the Colorado area to find opportunities that connect them based on skill, schedule or passion.

The guide includes opportunities for skilled volunteers, individuals, families, groups or youth volunteers, and features sections based on the amount of service required.

Guides are distributed during National Volunteer Week in April, in the *Sunday Denver Post* and at local businesses throughout Denver.

Metro Volunteers also produces a guide for youth 17 years and younger. This guide lists age limitations by nonprofit, if parents need to be onsite to assist the youth volunteers or sign waivers and if a young volunteer is allowed to volunteer with friends.

Source: Kristen York, Marketing and Communications, Metro Volunteers, Denver, CO. Phone (303) 282-1234. E-mail: YorkK@MetroVolunteers.org. Website: www.metrovolunteers.org

Identify Features and Benefits of Positions

Whenever you advertise or post a notice for a volunteer position, be sure to include both its features and accompanying benefits.

Example: Front Desk Receptionist

Features — Meet the public, answer questions, direct visitors to desired locations, answer the phone, some typing, other light duties.

Benefits — Meeting and assisting many people, learning about many aspects of the hospital, center of hospital's activity with visitors, learning phone and other procedures, increasing organizational skills.

Dos and Don'ts for Defining Volunteer Roles

Creating a volunteer job description is the first step for assigning the correct person to any volunteer role. Recruiting volunteers under a general umbrella of volunteer can lump too many individuals with varied backgrounds and skills into the same generic category.

Gather your volunteer management staff and ask the questions, "What do we want this volunteer to do?" and "Where is our greatest need?" These questions will allow you to define volunteer roles within your nonprofit.

Follow this list of dos and don'ts when assigning volunteer job descriptions:

❏ Do take time with your management team to define volunteer objectives and specific roles.

❏ Don't take the task of setting volunteer roles lightly. Volunteers bring a breadth of skills and services to your organization, so it's important to treat this task as critical to your nonprofit.

❏ Do create a list of volunteer roles including a task sheet that details specific expectations about the role for the volunteer.

❏ Don't create a list of impossible expectations. Be realistic about the time allotted for each volunteer role and ensure that the expectations of the role fit the time frame. Creating an extensive list for a 10-hour-per-month volunteer role will only ensure a feeling of failure by the volunteer.

❏ Do list the skills the volunteer will need to successfully fulfill the role. Are computer skills, people skills or technological skills needed? If so, be sure to include as much detail about the required skill set as possible to avoid assigning the wrong volunteer to the role.

❏ Don't ask the volunteers to take on the slush pile of work that staff refuse to do. Expecting a volunteer to take on the least appealing work is a recipe for disaster.

❏ Do review the volunteer job descriptions to ensure that what has been determined among your volunteer management staff is reflected in the job descriptions. Also, ask current volunteers to review the volunteer job descriptions and offer their feedback.

Volunteers Deserve Your High Expectations

The saying, "We become products of our environment," rings especially true in the volunteer field.

If your expectations of volunteers are moderate at best, moderate performance is the best you will ever receive. If paid staff exhibit mediocre commitment toward their jobs and achievement of goals, how can you expect volunteers to do any more?

Instead, create an atmosphere of high expectations for volunteers. Then watch them rise to the occasion.

To help your volunteers become all that they can be, incorporate these management principles into your work with them:

☐ **Show volunteers what is expected of them.** Have clearly defined objectives for individual volunteers, structured committees and boards. This includes job descriptions as well as quantifiable goals for the year or the duration of a project.

☐ **Enlist one or two leaders to help elevate others to** a new level of performance. Share your expectations with those who can help you motivate others. Ask them to focus their efforts on this task.

☐ **Recognize and reward those who are living up to expectations.** Whenever a volunteer demonstrates behavior exceeding your highest expectations, recognize him/her both individually and publicly. Consider offering incentives for those who meet incremental benchmarks as they progress toward stated goals.

☐ **Include volunteers and board members in the planning process.** If you want these people to own a higher standard of involvement, they should be included in shaping and determining objectives.

Expect great things of your volunteers. Model expected behavior for them. Be there to help them succeed. And when you see them meeting and exceeding your expectations, recognize them directly and through all appropriate.

Make Volunteer Programs Outcome-oriented

Just as it's important to evaluate the effectiveness of your organization's programs, it's equally important to measure those that are volunteer-driven to: 1) improve them, 2) affirm their effectiveness or 3) replace them.

Generally, each program should be evaluated annually and should measure outcomes on a quantitative and qualitative basis.

Here are some examples of outcomes you may wish to measure:

• **Individual and overall volunteer accomplishments toward stated objectives**: number of calls, amount raised, numbers served, contributed hours, etc.

• **Individual and overall volunteer satisfaction during the project**: attendance/absenteeism, results of volunteer satisfaction surveys, recognition, etc.

• **Effectiveness of volunteer recruitment**: comparative totals from year-to-year, number of new volunteers, volunteers per recruiter, recruitment structure, etc.

• **Effectiveness of volunteer retention**: comparative totals from year-to-year, changes in level of involvement/responsibility among volunteer veterans, etc.

• **Training effectiveness**: amount of time/materials committed to training, degree of staff involvement, level of volunteer understanding, etc.

Set Quantifiable Objectives for Volunteers

Whether you're planning a single project that involves volunteers or developing a comprehensive operational plan for the upcoming year, it's in everyone's best interest to establish quantifiable objectives for volunteers.

In fact, work with the volunteers involved to draft those objectives together. If volunteers are a part of developing the objectives they are more likely to own them and follow through with them.

Here are a few examples of quantifiable objectives developed for either individual volunteers or a group of volunteers:

• Recruit five new volunteers/members during the course of the year.

• Attend a minimum of 10 out of 12 regularly scheduled meetings during the year.

• Contribute a minimum of two hours each month throughout the fiscal year.

• Sell a minimum of 20 tickets per volunteer for an annual fundraiser.

• Identify at least three cost-saving ideas for the agency during the course of the year.

• Volunteer for at least one project without having to be asked to do so.

Examine what it is you most want your volunteers to accomplish, then break it down into achievable and quantifiable parts. They will be more likely to succeed if expectations are clear.

SETTING GROUND RULES: GOALS, EXPECTATIONS & USEFUL TOOLS

Help Volunteers Realize Challenging, Achievable Goals

As you know, people are motivated for different reasons. Nevertheless, most individuals are gratified when they make achievements. That's why it makes sense to look at each of your volunteer-related programs to determine what can be done to make it more goal oriented.

As you examine each program, keep these achievement principles in mind:

❑ Goals should be challenging but realistic.

❑ Include intermediate as well as overall goals.

❑ Include appropriate incentives and/or celebrations with corresponding achievements.

❑ Identify a variety of achievement goal types — those for individuals as well as groups. This gives everyone an opportunity to accomplish something.

❑ Allow volunteers input in determining challenging but achievable goals.

❑ Once goals have been set, monitor progress through regular meetings, updates in correspondence, etc..

People enjoy winning causes, so do what you can to help them win along the way.

Surveys Assist in Assigning Roles, Evaluating Progress

Obtaining volunteer feedback via survey can offer your organization an opportunity to expedite volunteer assignments as well as evaluate the volunteer program as a whole.

At Children's Home Society & Family Services (CHSFS) of St. Paul, MN, group and individual online interest surveys are an important part of gauging volunteer interests and assessing volunteer experiences. Shannon Broderick, volunteer services coordinator of CHSFS, tells us more about how CHSFS utilizes their volunteer surveys:

How does the individual volunteer survey differ from the group volunteer interest survey?

"Many of the questions are similar as they have to do with the basics of timing, length of commitment and interest, but there are also questions relating to the make-up of a group such as the number of volunteers and age of the members of the group."

Once the interest surveys are completed, what's the next step in the process?

"The potential volunteer is contacted in a timely manner (typically within the week) by a member of our volunteer services team to discuss their interest and what we have available to assess if there is an opportunity that might be a good fit based on their skills, interests, experience, etc. If a possible fit is identified, the volunteer is then asked to begin the application process by completing a volunteer application. With individual volunteers, we also ask for references right away to ensure they can provide those contacts. Upon receipt of those two pieces, we contact the applicant to set up

a time to meet."

What key questions are asked on the online volunteer surveys to help determine a good match for volunteering?

"Our survey is, for many people, the initial stage of the process. We ask questions about availability, area of interest and how long of a commitment they're looking to make to help determine if there are any opportunities that could potentially be a good match. We also ask how they became aware of our work or if they have a previous relationship with our organization. We use that information internally as we consider our recruitment strategies."

The CHSFS website also contains a Volunteer Experience Survey. How do you utilize that form? How do you go about addressing concerns raised?

"Interns and volunteers are sent the link to this survey at the completion of their volunteer experience and/or annually if they are a continuing volunteer. We use software that allows us to collectively evaluate the responses we get. If the volunteer expresses a concern or new ideas are shared, the feedback is discussed with the team on which the volunteer was placed. Our survey states that we intend to use the feedback to ensure positive and effective use of volunteers throughout the organization, and we do what we can to put their feedback to good use."

Source: Shannon Broderick, Volunteer Services Coordinator, Children's Home Society & Family Services, St. Paul, MN. Phone (651) 255-2444. E-mail: SBroderick@chsfs.org. Website: www.chsfs.org

Match Tool Aligns Volunteers With Assignments

For two years, Big Brothers Big Sisters of Puget Sound (Seattle, WA) has been using a volunteer match tool to link volunteer interests with available opportunities. The Match Tool, developed in-house, takes would-be volunteers through a series of questions identifying their desired time commitment and desired activities or hobbies to guide them in an initial match that best suits the volunteer's needs.

Rosalie Duryee, marketing coordinator for Big Brothers Big Sisters of Puget Sound, answers our questions about their success using Match Tool:

How has the Match Tool benefited your organization?

"The tool gives prospective volunteers a good frame of reference for how they might fit into our organization based on their interests and available time. We don't monitor the tool's use, but it's possible that the match tool has caused some potential 'Bigs' to better understand the time commitment and opportunities to be involved with our organization."

Did you develop the tool or did an outside source do so? What tips might you share with another organization who is considering developing a Match Tool?

"We developed it ourselves. It's a series of Web pages linked to selection buttons. We looked at the characteristics of each of our programs, and then made a series of questions leading to the correct result. Our goal was to create a short and sweet opportunity, and to show our volunteers that being involved with Big Brothers Big Sisters is really easy."

How often has the Match Tool been used?

"Our Web reports indicate the first page of the match tool has had over 1,000 hits since January 2010. Each subsequent page has fewer views, but users are at least checking out the tool."

Do you know how many matches have taken place with the help of the tool?

"At this time, the Match Tool is used as a frame of reference for prospective volunteers."

Would you recommend the use of a Match Tool for other volunteer organizations?

"Since we don't monitor the tool's use except to see how many people visit the Web page ... we can't say whether it's useful enough to recommend for other organizations. It is an asset to our website in that it provides another place to describe our programs and the opportunities available to prospective Big Brothers Big Sisters volunteers."

Source: Rosalie Duryee, Marketing Coordinator, Big Brothers Big Sisters of Puget Sound, Seattle, WA. Phone (206) 763-9060, Ext. 218. E-mail: Rosalie.Duryee@bbbs.org. Website: www.bbbsps.org

Use Letters of Agreement to Demonstrate Commitment

Do you utilize Letters of Agreement when enlisting new volunteers? Although such contracts can be simple in format, they are perceived as important by those who agree to sign them.

Letters of agreement are used by many organizations as a way to make volunteering more meaningful. When volunteers say "yes" to serving, the signed agreement strengthens their commitment to meet agreed-to stipulations.

How do volunteers react to letters of agreement? Many believe it makes their positions more official. The forms also demonstrate greater professionalism on the part of the organization and convey increased value of these volunteer positions.

Here is a simple volunteer letter of agreement you can adapt to your organization:

[Name of Organization]
Volunteer Letter of Agreement

I accept the invitation to volunteer on behalf of [Name of Organization] in the following way(s):

_____

_____

_____

_____

I will participate in the orientation program scheduled to take place on [Date/Time/Location].

I will attend a minimum of _____ of _____ regular meetings during the course of the year.

My volunteer term will commence [Month/Year] and continue through [Month/Year].

Beyond my specified duties, I pledge to serve as an ambassador on behalf of [Name of Organization].

_____   _____
VOLUNTEER   EXECUTIVE DIRECTOR

_____   _____
DATE   DATE

Agree On Project Outcomes Early On

When you have been asked or offer to take on a project, it's important that you discuss and agree on the anticipated outcome(s) of the project up front. Doing so will enhance the project's chances of success and diminish the potential for confusion or conflict.

What do you want this project to accomplish when it is finished? How will the agency or institution be better off upon its completion? What quantifiable measures can be used to determine the degree of success?

The use of a project-outcomes form can be helpful in identifying anticipated outcomes before the project begins and evaluating outcomes once the project has been completed.

ANTICIPATED PROJECT OUTCOMES

Project Name _____

Start Date _____ End Date _____

To be completed prior to project

Describe the goal of this project in one sentence:

This project will be deemed a success if the following outcomes are realized:

1.

2.

3.

To be completed at conclusion of project

The following were the actual outcomes of the project:

1.

2.

3.

Future project outcomes can be improved by:

1.

2.

3.

Motivating Volunteers: 109 Techniques to Maximize Volunteer Involvement & Productivity

UNCOVER WHAT MATTERS MOST TO YOUR VOLUNTEERS

Do you know what really matters to your volunteers — why they chose to devote time to your organization and not another, why they are volunteering at all? Understanding what fires the enthusiasm of your volunteers (and what grates on their nerves) is key to making the most of their time and yours.

Three Simple Tips for Volunteer Recruiting, Retention

Volunteers offer every service organization a valuable commodity and service. Recruiting and retaining volunteers can be simple with clear and concise communication. Follow these three simple steps to recruit and retain volunteers:

1. **Explain what's in it for them.** Be specific in how volunteer service assists your clients or your cause. Offer examples and feature current volunteers in your volunteer recruiting materials by way of testimonials from those served and those serving.

2. **Offer a clear call to action.** Clearly define the necessary steps potential volunteers will need to make before becoming a full-fledged volunteer. Be clear about the amount of training, whom to contact and how and the necessary next step.

3. **Make clear, achievable requests.** In your recruitment announcement, offer details and examples of the volunteer service needed at your nonprofit. Don't gloss over your need or miss important details or you'll wind up with dissatisfied volunteers.

Key In to What Motivates Volunteers to Match Them to Tasks

When you get a new volunteer, do you simply assign the person to the next available task, hand him/her a name tag and move on to your next duty?

Hold on — taking a few more minutes to get to know not just when your volunteer is available, but why he/she is choosing to be available, can result in a much more satisfying partnership for both you and the volunteer.

When enlisting volunteers and matching them with tasks, recognize the distinct difference between skills and likes. A volunteer may be skilled at something but would much prefer to do something else. Just because an attorney is skilled in legal matters for example, doesn't mean she wants volunteer assignments related to her profession. She may, in fact, prefer a diversion from her daily routine.

Key In on Personal Interests

As you nurture relationships with current and would-be volunteers, recognize and respond to their individual interests: hobbies, current events, heritage and more. Maintain a list of those interests so you can respond to them. For example:

✓ **Personal collections** — Do you know persons who collect matchbooks, posters or golf balls? Pick up these inexpensive items as you travel and give them to collectors to let them know you were thinking of them.

✓ **Historical or current events** — If someone has an interest in Civil War events, share articles with him/her as you run across them.

Smart Volunteer Retention Tips

All nonprofits need a strong volunteer base to succeed and grow. To keep volunteers coming back for more:

✓ **Treat volunteers like clients.** Consider treating volunteers as though they are clients of your nonprofit. Nurture the relationship as you would a client's — offering ongoing support, care and attention. Create an environment of value, valuing volunteers who value your nonprofit.

✓ **Create an environment of show, not tell.** Post photo essays on your nonprofit's blog or website to show your volunteer board members, trustees and staff in action. Such essays reflect to volunteers how important their work is.

✓ **Introductions are in order.** Introduce volunteers to a client or recipient of your services. Nothing speaks louder than the gratitude of those persons you help.

UNCOVER WHAT MATTERS MOST TO YOUR VOLUNTEERS

Volunteer Input Proves Invaluable in Building Relationships, Fine-tuning Program

Seek specific feedback from volunteers to improve your volunteer program for them, their successors and the clientele you serve.

Kristi Slattery, volunteer coordinator, Vision House (Renton, WA), uses a program assessment form for the organization, which provides transitional housing with integrated support services to homeless single mothers and their children as well as to homeless single men recovering from drug and alcohol addiction.

Shown at right, the form asks 18 questions designed to gain the most from volunteer responses.

Asking direct and thought-provoking assessment questions will help to better your volunteer organization, says Slattery.

"I have learned things through assessment about volunteers that I wouldn't have otherwise, such as what motivates them, what frustrates them, other volunteer opportunities within the organization they would be interested in pursuing and more," she says. "For me this feedback is so valuable in building a lasting connection and relationship with each volunteer."

Slattery offers tips for creating a thorough volunteer program assessment form for your organization:

- Make your assessment form specific to your volunteer program and organization. Request details about how the volunteer feels while volunteering within your organization.

- Ask open-ended questions. Avoid questions that can be answered with a simple yes or no. Open-ended questions will give you the detailed responses that truly assess the program.

- Track your responses to measure your effectiveness.

- Don't send out assessments too often. Annually is a good guideline for existing volunteer assessments. Ask new volunteers to complete assessments within six months of their start dates.

Source: Kristi Slattery, Volunteer Coordinator, Vision House, Renton, WA. Phone (425) 228-6356. E-mail: kristis@vision-house.org

Asking questions that require more than a "yes" or "no" response, this volunteer program questionnaire helps staff at Vision House (Renton, WA) fine-tune their program to benefit both volunteers and clients.

Content not available in this edition

UNCOVER WHAT MATTERS MOST TO YOUR VOLUNTEERS

Placement Questionnaire Addresses Volunteer Satisfaction

You and your staff invest plenty of time and resources into recruiting and training volunteers. But what do you do to measure their satisfaction levels or address concerns?

Volunteer services staff with Saint Joseph Hospital (Lexington, KY) use a one-page placement questionnaire to measure how satisfied new volunteers are with their assignments. Jamine Hamner, volunteer coordinator, says they developed the form six years ago after realizing they rarely saw many volunteers once they began volunteering, either because of the placement location or the volunteer's shift.

Hamner mails or e-mails the placement questionnaire, shown here, with a cover letter to volunteers two months into an assignment. She reviews responses and forwards them to the director or unit manager to which the volunteer is assigned.

"If a volunteer is not happy with his or her placement, we can notify the staff so they can work with the volunteer to make the placement better or we can reassign the volunteer to a more suitable placement," she says.

She estimates her office sends 300 questionnaires annually and sees about half returned, noting that the use of e-mail has resulted in a slight increase in returns.

Source: Jamine Hamner, Coordinator, Volunteer Services, Saint Joseph Hospital, Lexington, KY. Phone (859) 313-1290. E-mail: hamnerja@sjhlex.org

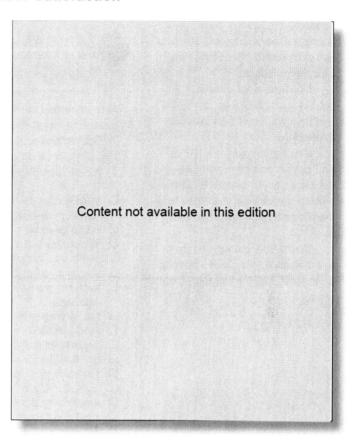

Content not available in this edition

Seek Volunteer Input Regarding Meetings

To keep volunteers satisfied about the way meetings are being run, seek their input.

To stay in tune with your volunteers' opinions about frequency and times of meetings, reimbursement of expenses and productive use of their time, use this checklist as a guide and add other items specifically geared to your organization:

❑ Are volunteers notified of the meeting agenda in advance so they are aware of items to be covered and know if their participation is really necessary?

❑ Is the agenda followed closely so participants' time is used wisely and productively?

❑ Is the frequency and timing of meetings acceptable?

❑ Is the designated meeting location convenient for the majority of attendees?

❑ When meetings coincide with regular meal times, are you providing acceptable food/refreshment options?

❑ Do meeting times conflict with volunteers' work schedules or standing commitments?

❑ Do the meetings still allow sufficient time to complete assigned duties?

❑ Do you credit time spent attending meetings toward volunteers' cumulative hours of service?

At the end of each meeting, announce the time and place for the next one. Demonstrate your flexibility and readiness to meet the volunteers' needs.

Retention Advice

■ Odds of retaining volunteers over time improve if you can diversify their experience. While some people like routine, most prefer variety to stay energized.

UNCOVER WHAT MATTERS MOST TO YOUR VOLUNTEERS

Discover Volunteers' Pet Peeves Early On

So much emphasis is placed on learning about volunteers' interests and strengths that we often overlook their dislikes.

Knowing what irritates volunteers when they join your ranks will help you quell their possible frustrations.

Use various methods to help pull out pet peeves — brief surveys and one-on-one visits. Share a list of possible pet peeves to help them identify and prioritize their own.

You'll find that we can learn as much about people by knowing their dislikes as we can from their likes.

EARLHAM Medical Center

TOP TEN PET PEEVES

Name_____ Date: _____

We're interested in learning more about your interests and likes, so we can match you with the most rewarding volunteer opportunities.

But we're also interested in knowing what irritates you so we can do our best to avoid those situations.

Please identify your biggest pet peeves by marking the boxes below:

❑ Meetings that don't start (and stop) on time.
❑ Public speaking.
❑ Not sticking to the agenda.
❑ People who can't remember my name.
❑ Having no say in the planning process.
❑ Not being recognized for my contributions.
❑ Asking people for money.
❑ People who have to control.
❑ Negative thinking.
❑ Not enough time to socialize.
❑ Too much socializing.
❑ Lack of staff involvement/support.
❑ Accessibility (i.e. location, too many steps, etc.)
❑ Hidden costs (i.e. parking, meals, travel back and forth, etc.)
❑ Dealing with finances.
❑ Inadequate resources to complete projects satisfactorily.

❑ Being asked to take on too much/spread too thin.
❑ Not being considered for leadership positions.
❑ Getting too much information handed/sent to me.
❑ Working with others who don't take their work seriously.
❑ Working with people I don't know.
❑ Disorganized/unclean facilities.
❑ Being treated like a child.
❑ Having no voice in assignments.
❑ Having to attend too many meetings.
❑ Feeling uninformed about the organization I am serving.
❑ Changing goals/direction after the project has begun.
❑ Lack of deadlines (no timetable).
❑ Unclear policies.
❑ Working with my hands.
❑ Others _____

Don't Misuse Your Most Able Volunteers

If you have volunteers who are expected to manage major projects, don't misuse and perhaps alienate them by assigning them petty tasks. Doing so has multiple negative consequences such as:

- Detracting them from much more important duties which, if not completed properly or in a timely fashion, will have a noticeable impact on programs.
- Under-utilizing their leadership and management skills.

- Demonstrating to others that it doesn't pay to take on big projects if you're also expected to complete more menial tasks as well.
- Burning out your best volunteers and diminishing their length of service with your organization.

Guard your top volunteers. Carefully weigh the consequences of each assignment.

Motivating Volunteers: 109 Techniques to Maximize Volunteer Involvement & Productivity

TRAINING & EDUCATIONAL PROCEDURES HELP TO ENERGIZE

Orientation and training are among the first and most foundational elements of any new job. Why should volunteering be any different? Engaging, entertaining and attention-grabbing training can sometimes be the difference between confident volunteers who are in command of their duties and tentative volunteers who are just getting by as best they can.

Entertaining Orientation Grabs Attention, Interest

Orientation meetings for new board members and volunteers don't need to be boring experiences.

While it's important for your new board members to become familiar with the goals, programs and history of your organization, learning about and discovering these things can be entertaining, informative and involve some friendly competition.

Try some of these ideas to make your next meeting of new board members and volunteers an anticipated occasion:

Trivial Pursuit — Use a computer graphics program to make cards, game pieces and a board so any number of players can correctly answer the most questions (both important facts and fun bits of trivia) about your organization.

Six degrees of separation — Take a family tree approach to an activity where new board members and volunteers create a chart, starting with how they first became familiar with your institution. Points can be earned by naming the most people who have been involved as supporters or for tracing family involvement back the longest.

Audio and visual flash cards — Make tapes and/or slides of various departments and activities within your facility, then see which new board member or volunteer will be first to answer which program or job is being shown. Follow the game with a brief tour of some of those areas and introductions to department heads.

Trolley tour and box lunch — If your institution has buildings in a widespread radius in the same city, or if you have a large campus, treat your guests to a guided tour as if they are visiting a new place with historic landmarks. Provide an old-fashioned portable lunch, either on the trolley or bus or in a pleasant setting at one of the sites on the route.

Present a short play — Use talented volunteers or staff who like to perform to give a fun recital with the plot revolving around historical events, current activities and future goals. Recruit your best volunteer researchers to gather facts, your best writers to complete the script, and the best amateur musicians, singers and actors you can find.

Even if an ordinary all-business meeting and facility tour is still required, your new board members will look forward to some unexpected fun with the hard work.

Create Interactive Seminars to Engage, Energize Volunteers

Don't offer the same old, same old when it comes to your annual volunteer training or new volunteer orientation. Instead, look for interactive opportunities at your seminars to engage and energize your volunteers while making them more likely to remember the important lessons learned.

That's what officials with Women On the Move (Boynton Beach, FL) and the KARS Consulting Group (Boynton Beach, FL) accomplished in summer 2010 when they collaborated to create a seminar tour to assist women-run and women-focused nonprofits, organizations and businesses in the art of grant writing.

The hands-on interactive seminar series teaches attendees how to create effective, compelling grant proposals and explore methods to garner support for their organization and ensure sustainability through the acquisition of volunteers, donations, fundraising and sponsorships.

To keep participants actively engaged during the seminar, event organizers implemented the following to create an interactive environment:

✓ Teams prepared elevator pitches to give to the class, which helped them with their presentation skills and ensured the audience's attention.

✓ Mock videos were created and presented to the class to keep the audience engaged.

✓ Abbreviated grant proposals were constructed by the teams and presented to show the audience how to proceed with this process.

✓ Individual interviews were conducted. Class participants interviewed each other which kept discussions lively.

✓ Teams evaluated one another.

Source: Leslie Harris, Women On the Move, Inc., Boynton Beach, FL. Phone (561) 200-0580. E-mail: info@mywomenonthemove.com. Website: www.mywomenonthemove.com

Help Fellow Employees Appreciate the Value of Volunteers

Helping colleagues understand the key role volunteers can and do play will strengthen existing volunteer-driven programs and make new initiatives possible.

If your employees recognize the contributions being made by existing volunteers, they may identify new opportunities for volunteer involvement in their own areas of responsibility. In addition, the more all employees recognize the contributions being made by existing volunteers, the more they will join in directing appreciation to them and, as a result, help to retain them.

Decide which of these practical strategies you can implement to help your employees better recognize volunteer contributions:

- Regularly list accomplishments/services of volunteers in your in-house newsletter.
- Make use of a volunteer bulletin board that showcases volunteers and their work.
- Invite a volunteer to speak during an employee meeting, describing his/her duties.
- Create a video — depicting your volunteers in action — that can be checked out by employees and used as a recruitment tool as well.
- Conduct an in-house survey that identifies new volunteer opportunities.

Teach Volunteers Through Role-playing

To generate enthusiasm and boost the learning curve at your next volunteer in-service, incorporate role-playing into training workshops.

Here are some ideas to make your role-playing sessions more effective:

✓ Have participants act out situations that have actually happened in previous years as a way to learn how to handle the unexpected.

✓ Have trainees critique each other's role-playing and offer suggestions for improvement. Be sure to stress the importance of pointing out what others are doing right as well as ways they can improve on their techniques or people skills.

✓ Look to your veteran volunteers to find those who have experience in training. Then have them conduct the sessions.

Strike a Winning Attitude Among Committee Members

What you are able to accomplish with committee members is often the result of a can-do attitude on their part.

To help them adopt on a can-do attitude, try these suggestions:

- Have a clear understanding of what you hope to accomplish.
- Help the committee understand how this project's completion will better the organization and those it serves.
- Be sure each committee member knows what is expected of him/her.
- Incorporate deadlines with each task.
- Follow up meetings with correspondence confirming key points and responsibilities.
- When obstacles arise, seek out alternative solutions and move on.
- Make time to recognize member accomplishments.

A well-organized and confident committee will achieve can-do results.

Combine Volunteer Appreciation With Education

The Lakes of Missouri Volunteer Program (LMVP), Columbia, MO, combines volunteer appreciation with education. In April 2009, LMVP staff organized a volunteer appreciation event that included speakers and presentations in an effort to promote volunteer education in addition to acknowledging the efforts of their ever-important volunteers.

Tony Thorpe, LMVP's volunteer coordinator, answers questions about the event:

How many volunteers do you have? How many attended the volunteer appreciation event?

"We have about 100 to 150 volunteers in our group. While we have 80 to 100 active volunteers with training, there are many more people who accompany our volunteers and assist. We're a statewide program, with volunteers spread out all over the state. At our volunteer appreciation event we hosted about 30 people, traveling from up to 250 miles away."

In what ways did you show appreciation to volunteers at the event?

"We gave fleece pullovers to volunteers who have been with the program for five years.... Our 10-year volunteers received binoculars.... We gave a husband-and-wife team who clocked 15 years a handheld GPS unit. We also purchased a few things and got a few others donated to hand out as door prizes. We tried to get a few nice items rather than a bunch of throwaway things. After every couple of presentations we'd break for snacks and coffee, then use the door prizes to get folks back to their seats. It worked very well!"

What educational offerings were provided at the event?

"We arranged for presentations, just like a conference. We had presenters from state and federal resource agencies speak on invasive species, fisheries and aquatic plants — a total of three presentations — a college professor talked about the influence of land use on water quality, a 12-year LMVP volunteer who works with a lake board talked about his experiences controlling inputs from the watershed, and the Lake of the Ozarks Watershed Alliance executive director gave a talk. University of Missouri (home of the LMVP) professor Jack Jones spoke during dessert. LMVP staff gave a few talks throughout the day concerning LMVP data, using the data for developing nutrient criteria and reservoir hydrology. We wrapped up with an interactive session regarding where the volunteers want to take LMVP."

What advice do you have for combining appreciation and education at volunteer events?

1. **"Involve volunteers in the planning of the event.** This was an amazing help! I handpicked a group of volunteers from across the state to assist in event planning. We had a sit-down lunch meeting one day and ironed out what types of presentations they wanted to hear, where we should have the meeting (important for a statewide project), how to best spend our budget, etc. I was amazed at how much more science these folks were hungry for. I had completely underestimated their ability to digest hard science. So, that leads us to the next point:

2. **"Don't underestimate the volunteers when planning the educational component.** As stated above, I wasn't prepared for how eager the volunteers would be to learn the hard stuff. In the planning phase we asked the volunteers what types of talks they wanted to hear and what questions they'd like to have answered by the speakers. They came up with some complex questions! We summarized their questions and gave them to the presenters early on so the presentations could be tailored to the event.

3. **"Start planning sooner rather than later.** Buildings may fill up and caterers might get booked before you can get to them, but even more importantly the volunteers' calendars fill up quickly. Many of our volunteers are retired, and I am always surprised at how busy retired people are! They are filling their calendars up several months in advance, and if you're not on there early, you get left behind!

4. **"Give them breaks during the event.** Whether to go to the bathroom or just get the circulation going in their legs, people need a break. And be sure to offer guests drinks and snacks, too. You'll find them gathering near the food talking to one another and making connections."

Source: Tony Thorpe, Coordinator, Lakes of Missouri Volunteer Program, University of Missouri, Columbia, MO. Phone (800) 895-2260. E-mail: tony@lmvp.org. Website: www.lmvp.org

Motivating Volunteers: 109 Techniques to Maximize Volunteer Involvement & Productivity

USE INSPIRATION AND INCENTIVES AS MOTIVATORS

Passion for a cause is the most common reason individuals donate their time as a volunteer. Unfortunately that vibrant sense of mission can be lost or obscured by the relentless press of frequently mundane duties. Refocusing on core commitments and conveying their power to volunteers in a meaningful way is one of the surest means of sparking inspiration and motivation.

Are You an Effective Motivator?

Motivating and respecting volunteers can be key to retaining your volunteer base.

"It's important to relate the volunteer's task to the big picture," says Dolly Fleming, currently executive director of the Community of Vermont Elders (Montpelier, VT), who has trained hundreds of volunteers in her 29-year career.

Fleming asks volunteer managers to consider 16 questions when evaluating their ability to motivate volunteers:

1. When was the last time you greeted a volunteer by name?
2. When was the last time you welcomed a volunteer to your agency by saying "Thanks for coming to help us today"?
3. When was the last time you treated a volunteer to lunch?
4. When did you last ask a volunteer how he was enjoying his work?
5. When did you last update your volunteers on developments in the agency?
6. When did you last have a special event to honor your volunteers?
7. When was the last time your executive director and/or board chair spoke to the volunteers?
8. When was the last time you said, "We missed you" to a volunteer who had been on vacation?
9. When was the last time you called a volunteer who had been out sick to see how she was doing?
10. When did you last mention your volunteers in a newsletter or in the press?
11. When was the last time you sent a personal thank-you letter to a volunteer?
12. When was the last time you called a volunteer just to say thank you?
13. When was the last time you sat down with a volunteer to evaluate his work, praise his talents and suggest ways to improve his efforts?
14. When was the last time you offered new opportunities to a volunteer?
15. When was the last time you asked your volunteers to suggest ways to improve your volunteer program?
16. When did you last ask volunteers to suggest ways to improve your agency?

Source: Dolly Fleming, Executive Director, Community of Vermont Elders, Montpelier, VT. Phone (802) 229-4731. E-mail: Dolly@vermontelders.org. Website: www.vermontelders.org

Learn to Muster Passion for Your Cause

It's difficult to address what we can't see. For instance, the employees of the organization for which we volunteer may be working toward a lofty goal that we simply don't know even exists. Or, there may be tremendous potential for achievement surrounding our particular volunteer cause, but we, and sometimes even the staff, don't see that potential for greatness.

It's like an enormous achievement that is waiting to happen but never does because no one can visualize it or know what a difference it would make.

That's where passion comes in. Your ability to reach down deep within yourself and muster passion for this cause — and to realize what is capable of being accomplished — can ignite a contagious spirit of enthusiasm in you, other volunteers, and even staff, that will cause people to give and accomplish more than they dreamed possible.

But at the root of any great achievement is a person who serves as a catalyst — helping others to see the vision of what could be, tirelessly staying focused on the issues that matter most.

You have it within you to be that catalyst. The dream is just waiting to unfold.

USE INSPIRATION AND INCENTIVES AS MOTIVATORS

Recognize How Children Can Motivate Adult Volunteers

What drives your volunteers? Your ability to discern what motivates each of your volunteers will help bring them to new levels of accomplishment.

Children are an often-overlooked motivator for many adults. It's amazing how some people will rise to the occasion when little ones are involved — as recipients of the good deeds, as young observers or as volunteer participants.

Involve children in any of the following ways, then measure the difference doing so makes among the adults:

- Have children thank volunteers face-to-face or with handwritten notes.

- Put a young person in charge of a project you know he/she is capable of carrying out. It will be difficult for adults to say no to him/her when asked to help.

- Have a youngster read and distribute volunteer awards. It will make the volunteers receiving the awards melt.

- As appropriate for your organization's mission and specific volunteer duties, invite volunteers to bring their children or grandchildren along to assist them in their volunteer tasks or as guests at your volunteer banquet or recognition ceremony.

Motivation Techniques

- Invite a client, patient, student or child who has benefited from your services to speak to volunteers or board members for a few minutes.

- Share unsolicited letters of appreciation with volunteers or board members by posting them, reading them aloud or reprinting them in your newsletter. (Be sure to get the sender's permission first, however.)

Give Volunteers Reason to Be Passionate About Your Cause

The mission of the nonprofit 5th Bridge (Northfield, MN) is to enhance individual and community life by encouraging the habits of volunteerism and philanthropy.

Staff accomplish this by offering opportunities that allow volunteers to support nonprofit causes of their choosing. Here are two ways they do so:

Volunteer Pledge Adds Commitment, Stability

In Northfield, the self-proclaimed town of cows, colleges and contentment, 5th Bridge staff developed the Utter Joy Campaign to encourage volunteerism with local Mooers and Shakers. Candy Taylor, executive director, says the campaign asks volunteers to pledge a minimum of five hours a month to the cause of their choice. To date, more than 1,100 volunteers have taken the pledge for a total of 68,160 hours of volunteer commitment.

"We want everyone to get all the good they can get from volunteering," Taylor says. "If you want to change behavior, the very first step is making a personal commitment, and that's what this is all about."

Creating a simple process to pledge has been key to the success of this campaign, says Taylor. Volunteers can take the pledge at the website and 5th Bridge staffers always bring pledge cards to events. A critical component includes gathering the volunteer's e-mail address so that 5th Bridge can keep volunteers informed of all available volunteer opportu-

nities and provide them with tools to assist them in fulfilling their pledge.

Goods for Good Promotes Volunteer Activism, Supports Local Need

In an effort that engages persons already active in 5th Bridge while encouraging newcomers, persons host garage sales at their homes or in conjunction with others at local businesses and agree to give at least half of the proceeds to a worthy local cause.

Taylor says this effort "helps local volunteers follow their passions" by allowing them the flexibility to choose the cause they would like to support. Also, it encourages and engages people who may not have actively volunteered.

In 2008, volunteers at 20 sites participated in the Goods for Good campaign, raising nearly $10,000 for a variety of local charities.

To assist with costs of maps, advertising and website updates, 5th Bridge staff ask for a free-will donation of 5 percent of proceeds or $25 from participants. At day's end, volunteers and organizers enjoy coney dogs and root beer floats sponsored by the local newspaper. Site leaders also turn in their monetary donations at the thank-you meal.

Source: Candy Taylor, Executive Director, 5th Bridge, Northfield, MN. E-mail: taylormail01@charter.net

USE INSPIRATION AND INCENTIVES AS MOTIVATORS

Create a Photo Essay to Show Volunteers in Action

A photo essay display is a great way to illustrate the importance of your volunteer program while saying thanks to your volunteers. By combining two art forms — photography and writing — a photo essay creates an eye-catching exhibit useful for volunteer retention and recruitment, acknowledgement and gratitude.

Try either of these two types of photo essays:

✓ **Narrative Essay** — The narrative essay offers a visual display showing a sequence of events or actions. The photos may depict an individual or activity over a period of time, showing and describing the events in chronological order.

✓ **Thematic Essay** — A thematic photo essay focuses on a central theme, such as volunteers helping at local food banks, and presents photos and text relevant to that theme.

Select one of these styles to create photo essays that capture the essence of how your volunteers are changing your nonprofit and the community. Use the photo essays to communicate effectively internally. Share them with your local newspaper as a way of acknowledging your nonprofit and the work done there.

Photo Essay Elements

A photo essay requires vivid photos of volunteers in action, plus compelling text to add impact. Include these elements in yours:

- *Story.* The photo essay should convey a story and the photos should be able to stand alone, without explanation or written text, and still tell a visual story.

- *Images.* Use a variety of photos. Include close-ups, wide-angle shots and photos depicting emotions to paint a vivid picture.

- *Detail.* Use detailed photos and concisely written text to tell the story and to reflect the essay's theme.

- *Captions.* Include captions with photos to add more detail, acknowledge volunteers by name and add to the story.

Seven Ways to Engage Power-motivated Volunteers

What strategies do you use to motivate volunteers?

When seeking to encourage and lift up your valuable volunteer force, it helps to first know what drives a specific volunteer to give of his or her time.

Some individuals, for instance, are driven by power or the opportunity to be a part of something big, while others may be driven by a sense of achievement or an affiliation with others.

When seeking to motivate power-driven persons, keep these points in mind:

1. Choose assignments that allow them to rub shoulders with persons of authority and/or to assume positions of increased responsibility and authority.

2. Provide them with opportunities that allow innovation.

3. Assign them tasks that allow them to teach or train others.

4. Publicize stories of their efforts in external and internal publications.

5. Find legitimate opportunities to seek their advice and suggestions.

6. Include them on your board.

7. Present them with awards and letters of commendation.

Five Ways to Motivate Affiliation Volunteers

Some volunteers are motivated by power. Others by a sense of achievement. Still others are motivated by being affiliated with persons or things.

Here are five ways to motivate affiliation volunteers:

1. Offer team volunteer projects.

2. Provide socializing times.

3. List names of persons involved with a project in printed materials.

4. Allow these persons to work with clients.

5. Provide recognition through affiliation: decals, lapel pins, business cards for volunteers, etc.

Recognizing that these persons are motivated by their association with others will help you identify more ideas.

Volunteer Perks

- Offer volunteers free meals when cafeterias or cafes are part of your environment. If you do not have on-site dining facilities, consider getting discounts or gift certificates donated from area eating establishments for occasional free meals, or having food delivered now and then.

Offer Perks to Persons Assigned Cleanup Duties

Who wants to be assigned to a clean up after a special event or quarterly luncheon?

That's no fun. Or is it?

Get your volunteers clamoring for cleanup duties by beefing up the attractiveness of such assignments. For example, offer a special incentive for those who serve on cleanup: taking home a centerpiece, going out for a complimentary meal following cleanup, free event admission or other privileges.

Five Ways to Connect With Achievement-motivated Persons

When working with volunteers who are motivated by a drive to achieve, be sure to:

1. Encourage their participation in goal-setting meetings.
2. Give them job assignments that offer increased responsibility.
3. Have top management acknowlede their achievements.
4. Seek out quantifiable assignments that include benchmark points of success.
5. Offer them the opportunity to provide input and advice and challenge decisions.

Volunteer Passports Encourage Participation

When it comes to volunteer incentives, think creatively. After all, a well-received incentive can mean the difference between having persons show up to help once and disappear from your radar or become committed to your cause for years to come.

A volunteer passport program is one type of incentive that can encourage volunteers to serve in various areas of your organization, stretch their abilities or fill needed spots at various locations.

Choose one or more of these ideas to introduce a volunteer passport program to motivate your volunteers:

- Create a paper passport that outlines various areas of service and hours of service needed in each to receive a stamp. For example, to encourage volunteers to serve clients directly, work in administrative functions and help with outreach activities, create a page in the passport for each area of service.
- If your nonprofit reaches different areas of your community or has several offices, make a passport page for each office where volunteers are encouraged to serve. To draw volunteers to your uptown or downtown locations, feature those locations and areas within these offices where help is most needed. Volunteers can earn stamps in the different locations and offer your organization better coverage.
- Create a passport that features abilities or skills volunteers can achieve while serving your organization. For example, to encourage volunteers to work toward public speaking for your organization or learn a technical skill, design your passport to reflect these skills of achievement. Passports can be tailored to each volunteer based on his/her potential. As volunteers become more skilled, stamps earned take them closer to their reward.
- To emphasize the passport/travel theme, reward volunteers who earn all their passport stamps with a travel-related item of value such as a trolley ride, all-expenses-paid trip in your town or region, gasoline gift card, bus pass or other creative incentives.

Once you have established a volunteer passport program, spread the word about it as yet another way to encourage persons to volunteer with your organization.

USE INSPIRATION AND INCENTIVES AS MOTIVATORS

Rules to Remember

- Remember the rule of reciprocation. When someone carries out an act of kindness for you, it's natural to want to return the favor. Do something nice for those around you every day.

Retention Tips

- Create a bulletin board or display case for your volunteers. Post accomplishments, list new volunteer opportunities and identify your volunteer of the week (or month).

Take Steps to Recharge and Keep Your Outlook Positive

A big part of a volunteer manager's job is to keep volunteers and the staff who work with them upbeat, positive and focused on working together toward the greater good.

Most days, this cheerleader role may come naturally for you. But what about days when it doesn't?

Do your part to stay positive and focused on your organization's mission while avoiding job burnout by giving yourself some breathing space now and then. Use these remedies as ways to gain perspective and break with routine:

1. Take one day out of each month to visit other volunteer-driven nonprofits. Discover what they're doing to recruit, retain and manage volunteers.

2. Designate at least one day during each quarter as chew-the-fat-day. Take other staff and key volunteers to a pleasant environment to look at the big picture and talk about what's working and what's not working.

3. Spend some time each week walking your facility or campus, witnessing programs and services in action and reminding yourself how volunteers are making a noticeable difference in the lives of those you serve.

Ever Considered Volunteer Levels or Clubs?

It's not uncommon for most fundraising endeavors to have giving levels or giving clubs as a way to encourage both contributions and increased giving.

Why not apply that same concept to volunteers? Why not establish levels of volunteerism with accompanying levels of benefits for those who contribute more time?

Those volunteers who gave at the minimum level of time during the past fiscal year, say one to five hours in total, would receive the benefits for that level. Perhaps benefits would include having their name listed in the annual report and receiving an invitations to the all-volunteer picnic held each summer.

Those volunteers who gave at the high-end level, say 250 hours or more during the past fiscal year, would receive benefits associated with that level of involvement. Examples might include:

- Dinner with the CEO and board.
- Two special receptions.
- Complimentary tickets to events.
- Preferred parking.
- Special volunteer business cards.

And the list goes on.

By providing top-end volunteers with increasingly more benefits and prestige, you're encouraging greater volunteer involvement and rewarding those who give the most time.

Motivating Volunteers: 109 Techniques to Maximize Volunteer Involvement & Productivity

WORK TO BUILD VOLUNTEERS' CONFIDENCE AND LOYALTY

Confident volunteers are volunteers who can be depended on. Loyal volunteers can provide years or even decades of cost-free service. Strategies offered here, like building meaningful traditions, offering meaningful advances in duties, instilling camaraderie and regularly and publicly expressing praise, can help instill these two critical qualities.

Instill Confidence in Newly Appointed Volunteers

Most great volunteers are made, not born. They require some training and education about your organization, but, most of all, encouragement and confidence boosting.

As an experienced volunteer manager, you are well aware of the resources and skilled peers available to aid you.

But put yourself in a newcomer's shoes: They have been asked to do an important job that is new to them, and they aren't being paid. They want to make a good impression and need occasional affirmation that they are on the right track. They may have had a previous unpleasant volunteer experience with another organization and were ready to give up volunteer endeavors for more lucrative pursuits or re-warding hobbies.

The way you work with a new volunteer may change his or her perception of helping others for the better. As a vol-unteer manager, your words of praise will carry considerable weight. With this in mind, here are some pointers to boost volunteers' confidence:

- **Be clear about your expectations.** Don't be too reluctant to ask new recruits to do a crucial task if you know they are well suited to the job. But do offer a specific outline of deadlines, persons to contact for assistance, and an invitation to call you directly if obstacles are encountered that may impede their efforts.

- **"I know you can do it,"** is a powerful remark and show of confidence. When possible, make favorable comments about their previous successes in the workplace or community. "We are so lucky to have you on board," and "This job is in very capable hands," will keep them inspired to not let you down.

- **Be unfailingly sincere in your praise.** Don't invent a compliment just for the sake of saying something nice. Keep your eyes open for an act genuinely worthy of praise, then seek out the individual to explain why you were impressed by his/her competence, kindness or diplomacy. "I noticed how smoothly you derailed that brewing conflict by offering another suggestion" represents one example.

- **Express your confidence publicly.** Each time you meet with your committee or group, note the newcomers and make positive remarks about them. If they have completed their first job ahead of schedule, obtained a new sponsor or contacted everyone on their calling list, mention these successes to the whole group. Your show of confidence will encourage others to join in with praise for the newcomer.

- **Thank them with a brief note or small gift.** The smallest token of appreciation, even putting a whimsical gold star sticker on their lapel at a meeting, will be a heartwarming gesture.

- **Be creative.** Make a short list of fun inexpensive ways to say thanks. Ask your board chair to send a personal note of appreciation. Produce a news release that speaks of your organization's "anticipated accomplishments with the addition of the following new volunteers."

Your attention to confidence-building will not only mo-tivate new volunteers to assume a more active role, but will also help you cultivate those who will one day rise to posi-tions of leadership within your organization.

Model Volunteer Success

Using a professional volunteer model can create a successful environment for your nonprofit. The ISOTURE model, cre-ated by Milton Boyce in 1971, stands today as a strong volun-teer model guide for any nonprofit. Consider using it to create a solidly built volunteer organization:

I = Identify where the right volunteers exist for your nonprofit.

S = Select the right volunteers for roles needed.

O = Orient volunteers to the organization and their role.

T = Teach them what is necessary to their role.

U = Use their skills effectively.

R = Recognize their time, energy and talents.

E = Evaluate their work and the program with them.

WORK TO BUILD VOLUNTEERS' CONFIDENCE AND LOYALTY

Maximize Volunteer Motivation

Many local affiliates of Americus, GA-based Habitat for Humanity International (HFH) operate their own ReStore, an open-to-the-public retail outlet that sells donated building materials, fixtures and furnishings at a reduced cost.

For the Greater Albuquerque chapter of HFH (Albuquerque, NM), it took one passionate volunteer, Ruth Friesen, to bring its ReStore into being. Today, the Albuquerque ReStore is so financially successful, it covers the Greater Albuquerque HFH's entire operating expenses.

Friesen shares tips to make the most of your volunteer workforce:

- If a volunteer wants to create a project — and has the passion to prove it can be done, along with the willingness to make it happen — say yes. "I volunteered for a year prior to opening the store, wrote a business plan, visited several other ReStores and scouted potential buildings," says Friesen, adding that she had not been specifically asked to, but did so on her own initiative.
- Suggest sponsorships, scholarships and contests from which volunteers can draw further motivation. Friesen

won a local Chamber of Commerce contest for the best business plan; part of the prize was publicity for ReStore through a local radio station.

- Do not fear your volunteers! Friesen says her greatest frustration during her yearlong project was encountering trepidation by the board of directors whose members feared they would sink money into a project that would fail, even though the concept had proved successful in other cities.
- When the time comes, say yes. "The board kept telling me to continue investigating for the entire year, until finally I told them if they couldn't commit, I had better things to do with my time," says Friesen. "At that point they realized they had a ready and eager volunteer they were about to lose, and that spurred the go-ahead." Remember, Friesen says, that an enthusiastic volunteer is one of your organization's most valuable resources.

Source: Ruth Friesen, Founder, ReStore, Albuquerque, NM. Phone (506) 217-0130. E-mail: rpfriesen@comcast.net. Website: www.habitatabq.org

Make Your Volunteers Feel Special

Don't take your important volunteers for granted. Let them know — often and in myriad ways — how special they are. Here are some ideas for doing so:

- Call them by name when you see them.
- Stop by to say hello as they work.
- Select a volunteer of the week, month and year.
- Provide volunteers with a suggestion box — and listen to what they suggest.

- Give them a discount on merchandise.
- Provide them with a free meal or gourmet coffee drink.
- When a celebrity or someone of note visits, bring him/her to meet your volunteers.
- Devote a bulletin board or other space to volunteer news.
- Get a business to sponsor the cost of several volunteer recognition perks — meals out, movie tickets, theater tickets and more.

Make Top Performers Feel Like Insiders

If you have volunteers or board members whose responsibilities and/or dedication make them an obvious cut above the rest, don't hesitate to let them know they're special. Doing so recognizes their talent and dedication and encourages continued commitment. You are grooming them for positions of greater responsibility.

Examples of perks for extra-mile volunteers might include:

- Seeking their advice.

- Inclusion at certain staff meetings.
- Designated parking.
- Listing them in the employee directory.
- Lunch with the CEO.
- Sending them the staff newsletter.

Will other volunteers balk at such special treatment? Perhaps a few, but more importantly, they will see that hard work and dedication are recognized and rewarded.

WORK TO BUILD VOLUNTEERS' CONFIDENCE AND LOYALTY

Strategies That Build Loyalty

Interested in building loyalty to your organization among volunteers, members, your board, and other constituents? These strategies will help do just that:

- **Build meaningful traditions.** Annual ceremonies — whether with pomp and circumstance or a flair unique to your nonprofit — contribute to the bonding process of those affiliated with your organization.

- **Instill camaraderie.** Building loyalty among colleagues and friends associated with your organization also strengthens agency loyalty.

- **Make roles and events official.** Make it important to be appointed to a volunteer or board position. Introduce and publicize new members or appointed individuals. Present them with a certificate or lapel pin as part of their entry into your organizational family.

- **Position your organization against the competition.** Although you might want to avoid doing it in a negative fashion, there is no better way to build instant loyalty than to position yourself against a rival. One potential downside: You may lose potential members who view you as someone from the other side.

- **Tug at the heart strings.** Invoke dearly held memories linked to past times with your agency or institution. Focus attention on a long-respected employee or board member for whom many have great admiration.

Organizational loyalty results in commitment, and commitment results in a willingness to contribute both time and resources. Examine ways in which you can work to build greater loyalty among your organization's constituency.

Lapel Pins Spell PRIDE

Does the organization you serve have an official lapel pin or one designated for its volunteer force?

If lapel pins are available, wear them regularly. They display your loyalty and pride without having to say a word.

If your organization does not have lapel pins, you might want to work through staff and offer to purchase a number of them as a special gift to the institution or agency.

Steps Move Volunteers From Short- to Long-term

What is your organization's method to retain volunteers after a one-time event? If your answer is, "We don't have one," you're missing a prime opportunity to turn short-term volunteers into long-term supporters.

Keep America Beautiful (KAB) of Stamford, CT — the nation's largest volunteer-based community action and education organization with a network of more than 1,000 affiliate and participating organizations — engages more than three million volunteers annually.

With this vast network of short- and long-term volunteers, KAB staff have found effective ways to move volunteers into a long-term position, says Matthew M. McKenna, president and CEO.

These methods include:

- **Organizing attractor events and positions.** "Design an attractive, fun and photogenic program meant to engage individuals' interest in short-term involvement," McKenna says. "Attractor events should encourage fun and not require any prior substantial experience, training or preparation." Examples include local cleanup and a nonprofit or education fair.

- **Scouting for the more engaged.** "Because most organizations need volunteers who are willing to accept responsibility and perform leadership functions, we recommend empowering volunteers to reach out and engage and recruit newcomers at the attractor event," he says. Disseminate organizational information and gather contact information from attendees.

- **Employing a nurturing process.** McKenna says you can cultivate a new volunteer's potential in several ways, such as offering additional work within the context of an attractor event; promoting ongoing volunteerism by bestowing an official title upon a volunteer or providing him/her access to equipment or materials; recommending changing the nature of a volunteer's work by offering opportunities that ascend in scale pending a project's completion; and encouraging volunteers to meet the organization's staff and committee members.

Source: Matthew M. McKenna, President & CEO, Keep America Beautiful, Stamford, CT. Phone (203) 659-3004.

WORK TO BUILD VOLUNTEERS' CONFIDENCE AND LOYALTY

Stay Tuned In to Identify Volunteers' Life Cycles

One of the primary reasons volunteers agree to assist an organization is because they enjoy contributing their skills and knowledge for a worthwhile cause. But they also have a variety of reasons for choosing your particular institution, such as working with their friends, having more opportunities to be assigned to jobs they love to do and identifying strongly with your mission and purpose.

When the combination of these reasons are well-balanced, volunteers may spend many years generously offering time and talents to your cause. But if these reasons change and they no longer feel a solid bond with the organization, their enthusiasm will likely weaken as well.

Because both your organization and individual volunteers are constantly active and evolving, changing or expanding in scope, a natural cycle of involvement typically exists between most organizations and their volunteers. And even if the volunteer naturally becomes less active, he/she will be able to pass the baton to a newer volunteer waiting for a chance to do the same with a different approach.

Realizing that the natural life cycle of volunteering varies greatly from person to person, consider these approaches to keeping the flow moving in an orderly direction, ensuring more seamless transitions as changes inevitably occur within the structure of your volunteer team:

- **Determine the length of service for key positions.** When you have an unusually talented group of volunteers together, ask if they would commit to a term of two to three years and train a replacement group during their last year. Your new group will have a strong background for their duties, and have time to see others in action that may be qualified to replace them. When lengths of service are pre-determined, no one will be offended when it is time for them to take on a different assignment, and may enjoy their duties more fully knowing that it won't be a lifetime commitment.

- **Communicate with volunteers who are especially valuable.** All volunteers are appreciated and highly valued, yet some stand out as gifted and innovative. They may have more than one skill to share, but still have difficulty finding a niche with your organization.

Work as closely with them as possible, even offering a five-year plan with the combination of variety and consistency they seek as a volunteer.

- **Establish both long- and short-term responsibilities.** Some volunteer duties, such as chairmanships of major events, fall neatly into a one-time category. A past chairman can then become an advisory chairman or honorary chairman. But other assignments benefit from consistency and prior experience. Ask volunteers how they feel about doing the same job more than one year — they may be eager to serve a second time after having learned the ropes, or they may know the job is not right for them. Making the effort to accommodate either preference benefits both you and your volunteers, keeping them satisfied longer.

- **Find a place for both onetime and lifetime volunteers.** Depending on their individual personalities and skills, some volunteers will be straightforward about how long they intend to be involved with your organization. They may have career or family plans that affect their length of service, hope to make contacts in as many organizations as possible, or want to offer the same skill to more organizations rather than doing many jobs for just one. Graciously accept volunteer help on the volunteer's terms. One person offering expert assistance on a one-time basis when it is most needed can be as beneficial as years of service by a marginally enthusiastic lifetime member. Both types are valuable, but for different reasons.

When it becomes clear that one of your volunteers has lost enthusiasm for your causes, no one is benefiting and efforts may even be impeded. Even though volunteer managers are sorry to see this happen, it may be only a natural part of that particular volunteer's life cycle with your organization. However, those individuals may be willing to continue to serve as an occasional advisor and asking them to consider this will leave the door open for them to return if they have a change of heart.

Motivating Volunteers: 109 Techniques to Maximize Volunteer Involvement & Productivity

INJECT TEAMWORK AND FUN INTO THE EXPERIENCE

The difference between environments of collaborative teamwork and environments of competitive self-interest is night and day. To strengthen the spirit of teamwork among volunteers and employees alike — and to inject that touch of genuine fun that so often makes all the difference — consider the following strategies, tips and suggestions.

Some Projects More Suited to a Team Approach

It's helpful to periodically examine all the ways in which you use (or could use) volunteers. In addition, there may be certain volunteer-driven projects or programs that may operate more effectively by creating teams of volunteers.

As you consider instances in which volunteer teams of two or more individuals would be appropriate, here are some of the advantages of the team concept:

- For many individuals, working with someone on a project is more enjoyable.
- It may be easier to recruit volunteers knowing their responsibilities are shared.
- With two or more individuals, one person can act as a safety net for the other.

- Multiple persons bring more skills to a project — they can agree to certain tasks.
- A project's likelihood of being completed increases with multiple persons involved.
- Veteran volunteers can teach rookies new skills utilizing the team approach.
- You can multiply opportunities for volunteer involvement by having more than one person for a job; and greater numbers of volunteers result in increased gifts, expanded community visibility and improved ability to fulfill your mission.

Examine opportunities for teamwork among your volunteers and board members. Ask for their input. You may identify new approaches that will enhance your efforts.

Pair Up Volunteers to Maximize Productivity

Many volunteer managers realize the benefits of pairing up volunteers as a way to accomplish certain tasks more effectively.

Paired up, volunteers can often accomplish more than if working individually. They can divide responsibilities, help one another meet deadlines, complement each other's strengths/weaknesses and likes/dislikes and have more fun completing tasks.

Give it a try.

Select a project and assign tasks to volunteer teams of two. Then consider incorporating any or all of the following ideas to maximize productivity from these volunteer duos:

- Create a competition among teams based on different criteria — those who complete projects first (or on time), those who achieve the greatest success, those who are most thorough, etc. — then award prizes accordingly.

- Structure your training sessions so one half of each team gets particular training in one area followed by training in another area for the other team members. In this way you will have trained each member of the paired

volunteers in a special area so that together, they can complement one another.

- If your paired volunteers are expected to make calls on others — for instance, on donors or potential sponsors — design a dual script for them. Designate one individual as the lead presenter and the second as the one who provides supporting, key information. One person may be charged with doing the asking and the other answering any questions.

- If your volunteers provide tours, train one to provide more practical information regarding facilities/services, while the other focuses on anecdotal information.

- Pair veterans with rookies to train new recruits and pass the baton.

- Allow spouses and other couples to work as teams — also consider parent/child or even grandparent/grandchild teams.

Retention Strategies

- Create volunteers teams of three — one third-year veteran volunteer in charge of the task, one second-year volunteer familiar with the task who will be in charge next year and one volunteer entirely new to the task.

If You Can Make People Smile...

Some people have the ability to bring about smiles on the faces of others. If you're one of those blessed with a talent for bringing happiness into the lives of others, use that gift to its fullest.

There's far too much sadness, anger and selfishness in our world. Your capacity to inject a bit of humor, to pay a compliment that turns up the corners of another person's mouth or to convey a pleasant nod of support will diminish negative forces and produce a more positive, comforting environment for those in your presence.

Never underestimate your ability to produce a smile on the face of another.

INJECT TEAMWORK AND FUN INTO THE EXPERIENCE

Fun Ideas to Express Your Gratitude to Valuable Volunteers

In what ways do you surprise volunteers as a way of thanking them for their efforts?

"Volunteer coordinators nominate an outstanding volunteer who has served at least one year. The county mayor recognizes the volunteer in a council meeting. They receive a certificate and a clock along with a copy of the declaration that was read by the mayor. These volunteers appreciate the recognition in a very humble way."

— Virginia Lee, Volunteer Program Manager, Salt Lake County Office of Volunteer Program Services (Salt Lake City, UT)

"If I hear of a special deed a volunteer performed, I write a SpiritGram, which is a recognition tool in our organization. The form describes the deed and is reviewed by several top executives in the organization. A copy is sent to the volunteer and posted on our board. As a reward, we mail them a 'free lunch' ticket for them to use in our cafeteria whenever they desire. The volunteers love the recognition and feel special."

— Cecilia Alonzo, Manager, Volunteer Services, Our Lady of the Lake Regional Medical Center (Baton Rouge, LA)

Volunteer Teams Tackle Major Projects

If your nonprofit is facing a multitude of projects, consider the team volunteer approach.

Officials with the United Way of the Southern Tier (UWST), Corning, NY, organize volunteer teams for its Day of Caring event, a day dedicated to completing community projects. In 2009, nearly 300 volunteers representing 35 companies participated in the event. For 2010, plans are for 45 volunteer teams to tackle 39 volunteer projects.

Kristin Butler, manager of marketing and communications, says the most important aspect of organizing volunteer teams is communication.

"For recruitment, we communicate with last year's teams via e-mail and communicate with a broader audience via Facebook, our website and the media," says Butler. "After the teams have signed on, we rely heavily on the team captains to relay information to their teams. It is crucial to communicate at least once a week with reminders about what is expected of them, schedules and updates."

Volunteer teams provide a valuable service to cash-strapped agencies. Nonprofit and government agencies do not always have the funds to pay for landscaping, maintenance, painting or other non-essentials, says Butler. When volunteers fill these roles, agencies are able to spend their time and energy on helping people. For the agencies, it is an opportunity to recruit long-term volunteers and make more people aware of the work they do in the community.

Butler describes how the volunteer team system works for the Day of Caring event:

- ❑ Teams pick themselves —individuals sign up for the project in which they are most interested.

- ❑ Projects are assigned on a first-come basis, and UWST attempts to ensure every team has a project they can feel good about.

- ❑ Teams are assigned dependent upon the project's needs. This year teams range from two members for a painting project to 12 for a larger painting project.

Source: Kristin Butler, Manager of Marketing and Communications, United Way of the Southern Tier, Corning, NY. Phone (607) 936-3753. E-mail: kbutler@uwst.org

Three Ways to Build a Stronger Volunteer Team

Volunteers can be a like-minded group of individuals who typically work well independently, but by fostering an environment of teamwork among volunteers, you'll find that volunteers in your organization will become even more productive.

Volunteers who find their service to be satisfying are more likely to become long-term, dependable volunteers. Here are three ways to foster a stronger volunteer team:

1. **Develop a volunteer mission statement.** With all volunteers, collectively create a document that states the mission and details your volunteer goals. Be specific and creative when writing the document that will be signed by each volunteer in your organization. Post the mission statement in a visible location where volunteers can often review and renew their commitment to your nonprofit.

2. **Call a monthly meeting that covers updates and new information for volunteers.** Make the meeting an event that includes informative and motivational speakers and creates camaraderie among volunteers. After the meeting, socialize or take the meeting to a social venue.

3. **Schedule an annual retreat.** Creating an opportunity for an annual retreat can be as simple as gathering volunteers at a local hotel for a weekend or one-night stay. Balance the agenda with unstructured time as well as structured opportunities to complete mandatory training or be educated on new efforts or techniques within your organization. Include opportunities for volunteers to relax and recharge by scheduling massage therapy, yoga or meditative opportunities.

INJECT TEAMWORK AND FUN INTO THE EXPERIENCE

Identify Volunteer Opportunities for Couples

Have you ever identified specific volunteer projects that reach out to couples, married or otherwise?

Inviting couples to volunteer provides this group with the opportunity to be together as they serve a common effort. It also offers a ready-made comfort level of knowing the person with whom each is working. More importantly, volunteering as a couple can be an enriching, relationship-strengthening experience.

The institution also benefits by getting two volunteers with each request instead of one.

Follow these steps to initiate a program that encourages couples to volunteer:

- **Assess your organization's volunteer opportunities to identify those that might appeal to couples.** Survey all employees to help identify couples' opportunities. Create a checklist of projects ranging from simple to more complex — filing, staffing the front desk, co-chairing an event, team phoning or solicitation, serving as hosts or tour guides, and more.

- **Develop a plan to market volunteer projects to couples.** Consider an ad program that reaches out to couples and lists volunteer opportunities. Recruit a couple to head-up your couples program and enlist others. Do a feature story on a couple already volunteering on your institution's behalf to illustrate the rewards of couples' volunteering.

- **Work with existing couples to keep them invigorated.** Once you have couples involved, find out which projects are most rewarding for this group and weed out those that are not. Ask couples what can be done to support their work.

- **Identify unique ways of recognizing couples' efforts.** Host periodic appreciation events for all couples volunteers. Offer special bus trips or discounts to restaurants. Make being couples volunteers attractive to those who have not yet stepped forward.

Test Ways to Make Routine Tasks More Fun

Bulk mailings, addressing envelopes, setting up and taking down displays after events are just some of the typically mundane jobs often assigned to volunteers. In fact, many volunteer jobs have routine but absolutely necessary chores attached to them.

But routine doesn't have to mean boring. Following are some tips for making routine chores more enjoyable and/or less time-consuming:

- **Offer a small incentive for quick work.** A little friendly competition can make jobs more fun for individuals or groups of volunteers. Rewards for speediest completion of tasks, such as a gift certificate, box of cookies or a gourmet loaf of bread, are examples of simple prizes you can offer.

- **Choose a pleasant location.** Invitation-addressing sessions or small meetings where routine business must be discussed will be more fun in a comfortable room, a lovely patio or someone's cozy kitchen. Offer a light lunch, tea, or a continental breakfast, depending on the time of day. Encourage casual working attire.

- **Hold a social gathering at a restaurant or coffee shop after the work is finished.** If volunteers enjoy meeting for a snack and conversation (as a reward for finishing the job), it can become a tradition after every business meeting or cleanup time.

- **Team people who enjoy each other's company.** Ask persons who get along well to work the same shift, and avoid pairing those who may have personality conflicts.

In addition, make an effort not to put slower volunteers together on the same task if time is an issue.

- **Combine tasks and festivities.** When possible, turn work into fun by choosing a festive theme for the activity. A potluck pickup party for cleaning up trash in a public park is an example. Let your creativity guide you to create fun themes.

- **Many hands make light work.** Consider trying to schedule routine tasks for a certain day of the week or month. Offer bonus volunteer hours or incentives for volunteers who show up to help on those predetermined days, or as a way to make up for missed shifts or assignments. Always have plenty of refreshments, supplies and sufficient work space available at these times.

- **Play pleasant background music or rent a good movie to watch during the task.** Many routine jobs require minimal concentration, so why not enjoy music or a newly released film that all would like to see?

- **Open any special attractions at your facility to your volunteers when they finish.** If your building has a swimming pool or fitness center, allow volunteers to use them on that particular day. They may volunteer more often if they like your equipment or resources when a free workout is the reward.

Finally, simply ask your volunteers what they think is enjoyable, even offer a modest prize for the best idea to make work more fun. Make a list of all of the input received, then implement them into routine meetings for the rest of the year.

INJECT TEAMWORK AND FUN INTO THE EXPERIENCE

Share Helpful Bag of Tricks for Volunteers

Offering tips and tricks for volunteers on your website is an ideal way to encourage interaction between volunteers and the clients your organization serves.

The Gifted & Talented Enrichment Services (GATES) Program at Bridgewater, Greenvale and Sibley Elementary Schools (Northfield, MN) offers all volunteers a bag of tricks to help nurture more fulfilled and focused volunteer experiences.

Working in small groups and one-on-one, these classroom volunteers help children from kindergarten through fifth grade achieve a higher level of learning.

Linda Kovach, gifted and talented specialist, posts tips at the school's website that can be used independently by volunteers. Here are some of the tips that your volunteers may find useful as well:

✓ If time allows, start each small group session with an attention-grabber (a puzzler, joke, team-building activity, thought-provoking reading selection, etc.). This activity is to get the students engaged immediately. An added benefit is that students will want to be on time so as to not miss the opening activity.

✓ Always plan for more activities than you think you'll need, so there is no wasted or down time.

✓ Always have something ready for students to work on if they finish their tasks before others do. This could be a journal question, a puzzler, an additional reading selection or anything else you find to be applicable. Students should be engaged in something worthwhile as they wait for others to finish and move on to the next task.

✓ To make sure everyone participates in the discussion,

give each student two to four small objects (choose one type: marbles, dice, dried pasta, self-stick notes or blocks). Each time a student shares, have him/her put one of his/her objects in a designated area. When all a student's objects are gone, that student is done sharing for that portion of the discussion.

✓ Have the speaker in the discussion hold a special object such as a squishy ball or other small, colorful item. This is a tangible reminder that only one person should be speaking and everyone else should be listening.

✓ Self-stick notes can be used by students to jot down thoughts they have while they are reading. These notes can then be referred to during subsequent discussions.

✓ Use Think-Pair-Share to encourage sharing of ideas. Ask the group a question. Give time to think of a response. Then have the students pair up and share their ideas with each other; after conferring with others, they may or may not alter their original responses. Finally, have pairs share their answers with the whole group.

✓ Use colored cups to get information from students. Choose two colors, red and green, for example, which fit inside each other. One way to use the cups is to have students keep the green cup on the outside and visible while they are working and do not need any help. If they need your assistance, have them switch the cups around to have the red showing — a nonverbal way to ask for help.

Source: Linda Kovach, Gifted and Talented Specialist, Northfield Public Schools, Northfield, MN. Phone (507) 664-3300. E-mail: Linda.Kovach@nfld.k12.mn.us.

Make Volunteer Projects Exciting Experiences

To attract enthusiastic volunteer participants and keep them motivated, assess each of your volunteer projects in advance and explore how to make them more festive and exciting for everyone involved.

As you examine ways to pack your projects with more fun, be mindful of the type of volunteer you're hoping to attract.

Here's an assortment of ideas to help you create your own fun-filled strategies:

1. **Convey a sense of excitement in recruitment brochures and ads.** Make it obvious that this will be a fun experience. List activities that volunteers can enjoy or benefit from during non-work periods.

2. **Build a growing sense of anticipation among those who will be participating.** Send periodic announcements prior to the event. Share the names of others who will be participating.

3. **Incorporate friendly competition with prizes and incentives for participants.** Pair up individuals or create teams for a more pleasant experience. Reward positive behavior with incentives. Offer inexpensive prizes that allow everyone to win.

4. **Pleasantly surprise participants.** To keep everyone pumped, surprise them with a visit from your CEO or board chairperson. Have a balloon bouquet delivered. Get a local choir to pop in for a brief surprise performance.

5. **Make your volunteers the center of attention.** Let volunteers know they're special by having a reporter stop by for a photo and human interest story. Invite your organization's employees to write notes of thanks.

Work to make each volunteer project a pleasant and fun-filled experience to keep your volunteers coming back for more.

Motivating Volunteers: 109 Techniques to Maximize Volunteer Involvement & Productivity

TURN POTENTIAL NEGATIVES INTO POSITIVES

Interpersonal conflict, negative attitudes, burnout, lack of focus, disorganization, compassion fatigue, inertia — you know the challenges inherent in a volunteering program, and you know the kind of impact they can have on both volunteer satisfaction and organizational functioning. Address these common difficulties — or avoid them altogether — with these time-tested approaches.

Use Upbeat Attitude to Diminish Conflict

No matter how great you may be as a volunteer manager, disagreement and conflict are going to happen among your volunteers.

Whether their beef is with you, another volunteer or someone else, one of the surest ways to diminish conflict and objections among volunteers is to maintain a positive attitude. Have you ever noticed how difficult it is to be negative or objectionable around someone who deals with issues in a positive way? A positive response to a negative statement is like letting the air out of a balloon. It eliminates the reason for arguing.

As you deal with volunteers, follow these guidelines for remaining positive and reducing the threat of conflict:

✓ **Make lemonade out of lemons.** If something negative has occurred, attempt to find the good in that situation and point it out to others.

✓ **Consider the source.** Some persons choose to be negative in any situation. Allow them to vent, acknowledge their frustration, then say something positive and move on.

✓ **Keep your eye on the prize.** When objections are raised or persons disagree about the way in which something is being done, ask everyone involved to step back and remember the primary objective you are hoping to accomplish. Doing so will make such objections seem less important.

✓ **Maintain a can do attitude.** Your positive perspective will be contagious, and any persons who insist on remaining negative will stand out like a sore thumb.

✓ **Praise others for being positive.** Recognizing positive behavior produces the opposite effect on negative behavior. When someone else is positive, point it out to that person. When a colleague demonstrates cooperativeness, praise his/her sense of team spirit.

✓ **Don't forget the power of humor.** While it's important not to make light of others concerns, remember that a little laughter can go a long way in diminishing conflict.

Your positive attitude will not only squelch the negative behavior of others, but will also enhance you as a leader.

Take Volunteer Care Seriously

At Hope HealthCare Services (Fort Myers, FL), a number of their volunteers spend time with people who are terminally ill. With this kind of often-stressful activity, volunteers could be at risk of a serious condition known as compassion fatigue.

Hope HealthCare Services is supported by more than 1,000 volunteers. During the organization's 30-year history, they have experienced no problems with volunteer compassion fatigue or burnout, says Samira K. Beckwith, president and CEO. She attributes that to proactive and preventative steps they take.

"We are very active in showing our volunteers the same compassion that we show to those in our care," says Beckwith. "Their well-being is our priority."

Here, Beckwith shares ways Hope HealthCare Services combats compassion fatigue before it becomes an issue:

✓ "Our volunteer specialists and staff members closely monitor volunteer activities through progress notes, phone calls and mentor calls," she says. "This is one way of identifying and alleviating any stress in its earliest stages."

✓ Volunteers are told they can say no to a request from Hope at any time. By monitoring their activities, we try to ensure they are not put in a position in which they will have to say no.

✓ After a stressful assignment, volunteers are encouraged to take time off for as long as they need it.

✓ Offering continuing education classes, such as How to Deal with Stress, as a preventative measure.

✓ Encouraging volunteers to have fun, through ice cream socials, coffee hour, brown bag lunches and our annual volunteer appreciation event. These are ways of demonstrating that we care, and it facilitates socialization, which greatly contributes to satisfaction as volunteers.

✓ Showing appreciation for what they do so volunteers know they make a difference — which she says is "the best way to help them avoid compassion fatigue."

Source: Samira K. Beckwith, President and CEO, Hope HealthCare Services, Fort Myers, FL. Phone (239) 433-8066. Website: www.hopehcs.org

TURN POTENTIAL NEGATIVES INTO POSITIVES

Techniques to Set Your Drifting Volunteers Back on Course

Finding talented people and persuading them to volunteer for your cause is a major challenge on its own. Keeping volunteers happy and productive is an even loftier goal.

Being sensitive to each individual's level of satisfaction can help in those efforts if you recognize some of the signals drifting volunteers project. Once you notice these types of signals, try one or more of these strategies to keep volunteers interested and active:

- Be sure they have assignments that suit their skills and talents. A people-oriented person may not complain about a job that requires little interaction with others, but may feel his/her true abilities are not being recognized.

- Are they paired with a more aggressive person who appears to run the show? If you are aware that a quiet person has been working closely with a more flamboyant type who attracts more attention, make a special effort to point out the accomplishments of the silent partner as well.

- Spend one-on-one time with those you feel drifting away. Invite them to coffee and ask for their ideas. This positive connection can lead to more successful interaction.

- Look for signs of personality conflicts with others on the team. The solution may be as simple as offering each assignments where little collaboration is needed.

- Are personal matters keeping their minds off of work? Even if they won't share details, let them know that everyone has times when they must focus on family or career matters, and ask how you can help them stay involved while offering more latitude.

- Evaluate if you are able to offer ongoing opportunities the volunteer seeks. Some people may be better suited as independent contractors with your organization. You may have an ideal one-time job for them but little else in terms of ongoing tasks. Encourage them to continue as contributing members or advisors with a flexible schedule.

- Visit with them about their goals and hopes for your organization. You may discover that their ideas and your mission simply aren't a good fit. If so, brainstorm to discover a particular duty that makes the volunteer feel he/she is helping to take your organization in a mutually rewarding direction.

Signs of Drifting Volunteers

Wondering if volunteers are losing focus and need help clarifying their purpose? Look for some of these revealing clues:

✓ They complete assignments, but not with their former level of enthusiasm.

✓ Meeting attendance drops off or they have other commitments to fulfill with other organizations where they may have more satisfying projects.

✓ Conflicts with other committee members or volunteers arise more frequently than before or maybe for the first time since they began to assist your organization.

✓ They no longer offer suggestions or ideas in group discussions.

- Have you done your part to make meetings efficient and convenient for the drifter? Their work style may be nose to the grindstone while yours is more relaxed and social, yet still productive. Try asking that person to handle arrangements for a particular meeting, then gain insight into his/her preferences.

- Do they feel appreciated and valued? Some volunteers prefer to work quietly and without too many words of thanks that draw attention to them. Others thrive on constant reinforcement and recognition. Find the proper balance for satisfying the potential drifter's needs without giving an impression of favoritism.

- Ask their friends for insight. You won't look like you're pressing for confidential information with a few discreet inquiries. A simple observation such as, "Liz did such a fine job on that event last year, what might be an equally interesting task for her this fall?" will begin a flow of information from those who know her outside of the organization.

- Let them know you view them as having a bright future with your organization, and that you have satisfying projects coming. They may be under the impression that they have done all they can, not realizing new challenges exist.

TURN POTENTIAL NEGATIVES INTO POSITIVES

How to Deal With Negative Attitudes

Although you may never get used to it, recognizing that anyone involved with volunteers will witness negative attitudes from time to time helps to deal with them more effectively.

What do you say to volunteers who make negative comments? How do you deal with those who complain about their assignments? How do you react to would-be volunteers who reject your invitation to assist?

Here are some techniques for dealing with negative individuals:

- **Stay focused on the purpose of the volunteer's involvement.** Attempt to bring the volunteer back to the primary purpose of his/her involvement. What are you attempting to accomplish? Focusing on the end result may diminish any negative comments or behavior.

- **Rely on a healthy sense of humor.** Interjecting humor appropriately can lessen an individual's negative attitude and help to avoid affirming such behavior at the same time.

- **Talk it out with a colleague or someone you can trust.** Simply talking about a negative experience can help overcome it. Don't keep it bottled up if it's bothering you. Get it out.

- **Don't dwell on negative experiences.** Put them behind you and move ahead.

- **Switch your focus to positive occurrences.** Rather than reliving the negative comment or experience over and over again, consciously refocus your thoughts to accomplishments, exciting plans or other positive thoughts.

It's easy to become soured by the negative behavior of others, but if we can somehow rise above those moments, our positive behavior will get us, and others, through the experience.

Curb Problem Behaviors to Put Volunteers on Right Path

Managing volunteers is similar to managing paid employees. Behaviors that follow employees throughout their careers can carry over into their volunteering efforts.

Checking references prior to accepting volunteers is one way to determine appropriate volunteer roles and help avoid problems with expectations. Another important step to success is to curb problem behaviors exhibited by volunteers.

Try these suggestions for correcting problem behaviors among volunteers:

Problem: Disorganized volunteers
Solution: Ask yourself if you have systems in place to create organizational success for your volunteers. Review your current organizational system and work with volunteers to improve it. Could forms be updated or revamped? Does the filing system need to be addressed for more effective use? Ensure volunteers understand reasons behind required steps to motivate them to stay organized. Ask volunteers for input to create a system useful to them and efficient for the nonprofit.

Problem: Unfocused volunteers
Solution: For volunteers who cannot remain focused and like to juggle too many tasks at once, provide a daily duty sheet. The duty sheet should act as a checklist that volunteers can follow line by line. Once the first task is complete, they move on to the next, avoiding problems with jumbled multitasking. If you are dealing with volunteers who get more chatting done than volunteering, find a role where they can interact by helping clients rather than other volunteers. If this doesn't work, offer them a role that involves a great deal of phone work or limits their access to others who may find their chatter distracting.

Problem: Chronically late or unreliable volunteers
Solution: Address chronically late volunteers or those who frequently miss assigned days in a serious but professional manner. Implement a three-tier behavior correction approach using a verbal warning, plan of action and follow-up. Work with the volunteers to address the behavior and create a plan of action to improve the problem. If the behavior persists, put such volunteers on drop-in status rather than placing them on the regular volunteer schedule to avoid being shorthanded.

TURN POTENTIAL NEGATIVES INTO POSITIVES

Avoid These Volunteer Turnoffs

As important as it is to set an example for your fellow volunteers and board members, it's equally important to avoid behaviors that could make their volunteer experience frustrating.

Be sure to avoid these turnoffs as you work with your colleagues:

1. **Dates that change.** Once dates for meetings and events have been set, don't change them. People oftentimes sacrifice to get volunteer commitments on their calendars. Changing those dates makes scheduling even more difficult and encourages others to question the meeting's importance.

2. **Not knowing the purpose and expectations of a project.** When scheduling a meeting or event, be sure everyone knows its purpose and what will be expected of them in advance. No one likes to be ill-prepared for a volunteer project.

3. **Unorganized meetings.** Keep meetings on track. Begin and end them on time, and follow an agenda closely.

4. **Individuals who impede progress.** Don't allow one person's behavior to ruin the experience for everyone else. If someone is too argumentative or controlling, be willing to address it for the sake of the others.

5. **Meaningless responsibilities.** Don't call people together to simply inform or entertain them. Make their time count for something that they find consequential.

Reduce Compassion Fatigue While Strengthening Resilience

If your organization's mission puts your volunteers, your staff, and even yourself into highly stressful situations, be on the lookout for signs of compassion fatigue.

Compassion fatigue is the extreme state experienced by those helping others in distress and preoccupation with the suffering of those they are helping to the point of traumatizing the volunteer or helper. It can be a common ailment among volunteers who work with clients dealing with traumatic events, health issues or animal welfare.

Kim Heinrichs, executive director of volunteer resources at San Diego Hospice and The Institute for Palliative Medicine (San Diego, CA), shares signs her organization uses to determine if someone is experiencing compassion fatigue:
- Inability to define healthy boundaries.
- Desire or need to fix patients' problems.
- Hesitation to share volunteer intervention with staff team members.
- Believing that patient can't survive without his/her help.
- Feeling of hopelessness as though nothing he/she does will make anything better.

Heinrichs shares steps to go from compassion fatigue to professional resilience:
- Take a break between patient or client assignments.
- Participate in supportive supervision meetings and volunteer continuing education and accept support from volunteer staff or coordinator.
- Discover and commit to personal self-care, including exercise, gardening, meditation or other forms of relaxation.
- Emphasize open communication between volunteer and staff to tackle potential patient or family challenges before they become a problem.

"Managers must understand that burnout is real and exists for both volunteers and staff," Heinrichs says. "Commit to best training and support practices by using training modules, available from national organizations such as the National Hospice and Palliative Care Organization (Alexandria, VA) and Volunteering in America (Washington, D.C.)." She recommends training modules that incorporate key topics such as saying goodbye, compassionate listening, boundary issues and best practices to educate and support volunteers.

Finally, Heinrichs says, be approachable and understanding so volunteers will seek help from the management team. Facilitate clear, ongoing communication between volunteer coordinators by instituting check-in calls to ensure safe, open dialogue.

Source: Kim Heinrichs, Executive Director of Volunteer Resources, San Diego Hospice and The Institute for Palliative Medicine, San Diego, CA. Phone (619) 278-6458.
E-mail: KHeinrichs@SDHospice.org. Website: www.sdhospice.org

Keep Volunteer Inertia at Bay

Without flexibility built into your volunteer program, your volunteers can feel their duties are becoming stagnant and they may consider looking for opportunities elsewhere. Don't let that happen!

Here are a few ideas to keep your volunteers excited about and engaged with your organization:

✓ **Build latitude into guidelines and policies.** Yes, volunteers need to have boundaries. They also need the opportunity to be creative, and, in some cases, to fail. They need to know that you have faith in them either way.

✓ **Ask their opinions.** Whether with a well-timed survey, focus group or one-on-one conversations, ask volunteers' opinions and ideas. Listen to your volunteers and you may be surprised by what you hear.

✓ **Revisit their commitment with them.** Persons may sign up to do one thing for your organization, but eventually realize they'd like to do something else. Or their life circumstances may change. Check in with them from time to time to see if they still feel well-matched.

✓ **Ask questions.** Specifically, ask what you can do to help them in their role and then follow through with appropriate actions.

Seven Ways to Combat Volunteer Burnout

Volunteers are the lifeblood of many nonprofit organizations. But volunteers, just like paid employees, can suffer from over scheduling, lack of direction, lack of motivation and other factors that can lead to burnout.

Here are seven ideas to keep volunteers motivated, positive, energized and connected to your organization:

1. **Prepare schedules that offer short stints of service** (e.g., four hours or less. Being able to offer time in smaller increments, volunteers are less likely to feel overwhelmed by their duties.

2. **Offer clear goals and direction.** Don't leave volunteers to flounder and have to figure things out on their own. Prepare a reference manual to assist with day-to-day tasks and offer training appropriate to the volunteer role.

3. **Offer vacations or leaves of absence.** Remember that volunteers have commitments and responsibilities beyond your cause. Insist that volunteers take time off as a sched-uled vacation to allow them to regroup and come back to your organization refreshed.

4. **Locate training opportunities** within and outside your organization for volunteers to raise their skill level while helping them feel more positive and energized by your organization.

5. **Promote work quality, not quantity.** Ask volunteers to perform tasks with care, then enable them to do so. Give volunteers manageable tasks that they can competently complete during their assigned shifts.

6. **Provide services or contacts** to assist volunteers with emotional overload. Prepare a list of resources where volunteers may get assistance with concerns, time management or emotional stress.

7. **Take a break!** Have staff take coffee or lunch breaks with volunteers to ensure volunteers feel part of the team and give the entire staff a breather.

Prodding the 'Foot-dragging' Volunteer

How do you handle those volunteers who continually drag their feet as you approach a deadline? What can be done to convince them to finish their task on time? Try either of these techniques, but know that the first will be to your long-term advantage:

1. **Incentives/rewards** — Offer an inexpensive but treasured item to those who finish by a certain date. Make everyone aware that this group will be publicly recognized.

2. **Avoiding negative consequences** — Encourage volunteer leaders to come up with peer-created consequences for those who don't follow through. Although you may lose volunteers who become embarrassed by such methods, this peer-driven method helps to diminish any bad feelings toward staff or the organization.

Motivating Volunteers: 109 Techniques to Maximize Volunteer Involvement & Productivity

RECOGNITION AND APPRECIATION MEASURES

If recognition and thanks are meaningful in the work you do in your position, imagine how much more important they are to those donating their time free of charge. By deliberately and regularly demonstrating to volunteers how much their work matters, leaders can maintain exceptional levels of enthusiasm, commitment and motivation.

Recognize and Celebrate Your Volunteers Every Day

Volunteer recognition traditionally occurs at an annual event. But don't ignore opportunities the other 364 days of the year. Here are a few suggestions to honor volunteers:

- Put up a bulletin board in your lobby or front office. Fill it with photos of volunteers in action and letters from constituents affected by their service.
- Invite the volunteers to a staff meeting.
- When they arrive for their shift, greet individuals by name and thank them for coming. When they leave, ask how their shift went and thank them again.
- If your volunteers use a touch-screen computer to check in and out, send customized greetings to thank and recognize the volunteers for their accomplishments.
- Schedule time in your day to meet with your volunteers.
- Greet them with a smile, handshake, hug or a pat on the back.
- Surprise the volunteers with fun treats and surprises (e.g., snacks, lottery tickets, ice cream, freebies).
- Compliment the volunteer in public.
- Write thank-you notes.

- Make regular phone calls to just say hi.
- Visit various work sites to interact with the volunteers.
- Show an interest in their health, hobbies and family.
- Encourage staff to call to say how much they appreciate the volunteers' service.
- Feature volunteers on your organization's website with a picture and a story on what they do to make a difference in the community.
- Make it a point to remember every volunteer's name and use it when interacting.
- Send a note or card to celebrate a special event (e.g., birthday, anniversary) or let them know you are thinking of them at a difficult time (e.g., if they or a loved one are in the hospital, death in the family). Encourage your CEO to send a note as well.
- Buy them lunch.

Whether doing so means putting reminders in your planner or placing self-stick notes on your computer monitor, constantly remind yourself to make daily recognition a habit rather than something that is easily overlooked.

Offer Your Volunteers Symbols of Gratitude

Make your volunteers feel special with these symbols of your appreciation:

- ❑ **Group photo:** Frame a group photo of all current volunteers with the front row holding a poster, complete with the organization's logo, displaying the year. Take this photo each year at the same time and distribute to your current volunteer base. Don't forget to display a large copy of the photo in your lobby or reception area.
- ❑ **Another group photo:** Organize a group photo of willing clients of your organization holding a large thank-you poster. Give a copy to each volunteer. This added

touch will mean a lot to your steadfast volunteers.

- ❑ **Thank-you card:** Each year, have all staff and management sign thank-you cards for each volunteer (or volunteer group/team). Request that each person add a personal, heartfelt note specific to that volunteer/volunteer group.
- ❑ **Invitation:** Invite individual volunteers to join in on a coffee break or casual continental breakfast with the head of the organization. If possible, create small-group opportunities for volunteers to attend a coffee with the head of the organization monthly or quarterly on a rotating basis.

RECOGNITION AND APPRECIATION MEASURES

Stewarding Volunteers: Special Ways to Say Thanks

Whether it's time for your annual volunteer recognition event or you simply want to show your appreciation on the spur of the moment, here are creative ways to thank your valuable volunteers:

- **Feed them.** Prepare a boxed dinner complete with all the dry ingredients and a recipe for an easy meal they can prepare for their family or themselves on a busy night. Wrap the box and include a clock tag saying, "Thanks for the gift of your time."

- **Write them.** When it comes time to collect volunteer time sheets, make an even exchange. Give volunteers a note of thanks from you, a staff member or from someone served by your organization.

- **Use others' words to tell them.** Creatively arrange, in a scroll format, quotes from your executive director, board members and staff about the value of volunteers. Tie printed scrolls with ribbons and present them to your volunteers.

- **Share comfort foods.** Collect recipes from each volunteer, inviting them to include personal stories about the

recipe, and assemble in a cookbook format. Include a personalized thank you from you and/or the executive director as the introduction.

- **Offer small tokens of thanks.** Give any of these small tokens with a clever message, such as:

  ✓ A brightly colored permanent marker with a note saying, "You've made a lasting and permanent contribution to our organization!"

  ✓ A $100,000 Grand candy bar with the note, "Just to let you know, your service is priceless to this organization."

  ✓ A ruler/tape measure with the message, "It's easy to measure the difference you've made in our organization — you're amazing!"

  ✓ A shirt with a note, "We know you'd give the shirt off your back… so here's an extra one for the next time you give your all."

  ✓ A bottle of sparkling apple juice with the message, "Cheers to a super volunteer!"

Recognize Volunteers Every Step of the Way

At the Seattle Aquarium (Seattle, WA), volunteers are not only recognized for years of service, but hours of service.

Each and every milestone of service is rewarded with a variety of perks and the listing of the volunteer's name in the organization's newsletter, the All Wet Gazette.

"Some volunteers are with us for years, but can only *"By recognizing volunteers* give a few hours, while others *at the small levels, you set* can give a lot of hours but may *them up to stay with you."* not serve more than five or 10 years — we recognize both hours and years served," says Sue Donohue Smith, guest experience manager.

At the aquarium, volunteers serving 100, 250, 500, 1,000 and every 1,000 hours after receive a certificate in appreciation of their efforts and recognition in the newsletter.

In addition, volunteers who have reached their first 100 hours of service receive a patch for their uniform. They then receive rockers, which are smaller patches that fit around the large patch that signify different jobs, every five years of service and every 1,000 hours of service. Also, all

volunteers receive pins for every year of service, with each pin portraying a different animal.

All volunteers receive the monthly newsletter and Weekly Critter News publications as a perk, as well as invitations to socials and picnics including the Dive Social and Exotic Team picnic.

Volunteers are also invited to staff meetings to instill their importance to the organization, and receive one entrance ticket for every 25 hours served, plus a free family membership after six months of service.

"By recognizing volunteers at the small levels, you set them up to stay with you," says Donohue Smith. "The bottom line is that volunteers at the Seattle Aquarium know they are important and critical to our success. They learn this on day one and it is reinforced to them constantly."

Follow the lead of the Seattle Aquarium, recognize your volunteers at every milestone no matter how big or small.

Source: Sue Donohue Smith, Guest Experience Manager, Seattle Aquarium, Seattle, WA. Phone (206) 399-7033.
E-mail: sue.donohue-smith@seattle.gov

RECOGNITION AND APPRECIATION MEASURES

Annual Garden Celebration Features Volunteer Display

Look for ways to jazz up traditional volunteer events as a way to thank those who serve and celebrate your volunteer-based organization.

To honor the volunteers who serve at St. Joseph's Health Centre Foundation (Guelph, Ontario, Canada), Volunteer Coordinator Carol McGuigan plans a luncheon.

The outdoor appreciation event relies on good weather and strong attendance of its 50 to 80 volunteers to make for a successful event held in the garden.

The theme "Volunteers ... Caring, Sharing and Growing," is fitting for the garden celebration, McGuigan says.

As a special tribute, McGuigan creates a display that greets volunteers upon their arrival at the event. Located at the entrance of the garden, McGuigan fills the board with photos of volunteers in action throughout the year and adds inspirational quotes that will move the guests.

Follow these guidelines to prepare a display at your next volunteer appreciation event — the volunteers will feel special for the time and effort you put into it:

- Prepare a three-panel, table-top display board approximately 6x4 feet, allowing ample room to display your message.
- Use brightly colored graphics, fonts and borders with a garden theme, or a theme that matches your event, to give a cheerful and fun appearance.
- Keep in mind this special group's importance as the display is being prepared, creating a message of appreciation. This luncheon is devoted to your hardworking volunteers for their efforts!

Source: Carol McGuigan, Volunteer Coordinator, St. Joseph's Health Centre Foundation, Guelph, Ontario, Canada. Phone (519) 767-3424. E-mail: cmcguiga@sjhcg.ca. Website: www.sjhcg.org

Five Effective Volunteer Appreciation Ideas

Without a doubt, volunteers are an invaluable resource to your nonprofit organization. Try these simple ways to show your valued volunteers exactly how much they mean to your organization:

- ✓ Frame a photo of the volunteer in action serving clients or helping your organization, along with a handwritten thank-you note mounted within the frame.
- ✓ Create a giant banner of thanks to include the names of all volunteers and handwritten greetings from staff, clients and visitors.

- ✓ Ask a school class to adopt your nonprofit and create a poster about the service of volunteers to post for your volunteers to enjoy.
- ✓ Ask a community leader to take a special volunteer to lunch in appreciation of his or her selfless efforts for your cause.
- ✓ Gather all volunteers and staff to join in an impromptu round of applause for a job well done by a specific volunteer or group of volunteers who have recently completed or are in the middle of a major project or difficult task.

Appreciation Event Celebrates Volunteer Accomplishments

Each year 2,000 volunteers lend a hand at Meals on Wheels Greenville County (Greenville, SC). The organization says thanks with an annual volunteer appreciation event.

The most recent event, titled 2009 Breakfast of Champions — Everyday People, Extraordinary Accomplishments, featured "The Biggest Loser" contestant Amy Parham, who spoke of great things ordinary people can accomplish with determination and hard work.

"There are so many heroes — fireman, soldiers, policemen, doctors and unsung heroes like our volunteers, everyday people who do extraordinary things," says Jan Dewar, director of volunteer services, explaining the event's theme.

Dewar shares her tips for hosting a successful volunteer appreciation event:

- ✓ Host an appreciation breakfast to allow for the most volunteers to attend.

- ✓ Draw a well-known, inspirational speaker. Find out who within your organization knows someone willing to address your volunteers. Think outside the box to determine who within your community could address volunteers in an inspirational way.
- ✓ Organize a committee led by a passionate employee who will put in the time to create an appreciation event that relays how important volunteers are. Shelley DiMarco, food service manager, headed up Meals on Wheels' most recent event, overseeing a committee that solicited door prizes.
- ✓ Provide items for volunteers to take home. Attendees of the Meals on Wheels event received a canvas bag, bottled water, hand sanitizer and a pen.

Source: Jan Dewar, Director of Volunteer Services, Meals on Wheels Greenville County, Greenville, SC. Phone (864) 233-6565. E-mail: janice@mowgvl.org. Website: www.mealsonwheelsgreenville.org

RECOGNITION AND APPRECIATION MEASURES

Host a Volunteer Picnic

An outdoor picnic is a relaxed way to thank volunteers and their families for the work they do. Depending on your attendees' ages, interests and numbers, consider:

- **A French country theme** with crusty breads, cheeses, fruits and wine in a beautiful and fragrant garden.

- **An informal tailgate party** in a park, at a lake or even in the parking lot of your organization, with prizes for the best tailgate food.

- **Poolside picnic** at a country club or home — your organization provides the food and catering staff.

- **Nothing but desserts** that are cool, refreshing and lavish. Have vegetables and dip or crackers and cheese for those without a sweet tooth.

- **An ant-free picnic fundraiser** where you create elegant picnic baskets of varying size, depending upon the size of the donation, then deliver to donors' offices or homes.

- **Celebration of cultures** featuring foods from area ethnic food establishments or volunteers' favorite recipes.

- **A day at the state fair** theme with a pie baking contest with ribbons, barbecues, carnival games, talent contest, live music or a pet show with prizes.

- **Progressive picnic** that begins with sandwiches and chips, then moves to one or two additional locations for heartier dinner fare, followed by dancing and desserts.

- **Vote for your favorites!** Create a ballot-type invitation where guests vote for their favorite picnic fare in advance, then enjoy eating the top choices when they arrive.

- **Midnight snack picnic** with traditional late-night foods such as ice cream, pizza, popcorn and cheeses held late in the evening, allowing guests to mingle and graze.

- **Go on a cruise** and bring the buffet! Have a nautical theme in decorations and casual attire, drinks with umbrellas (non-alcoholic versions, too).

- **Kids rule picnic!** Imagine the fun if the menu includes preschoolers' top 10 most popular choices combined with a contest where young guests vote on the best comedy routine performed by a parent or group of adults.

Four Easy Holiday Volunteer Recognition Ideas

Try these simple, effective ways to honor the work your volunteers do during the holiday season:

1. **Ask board members to write letters or cards to volunteers.** Divide the list of volunteer names among the board along with bullet points of ways the volunteer serves your nonprofit to assist the board member in writing a meaningful message.

2. **Create a "catered" affair with staff bringing dishes for a potluck honoring volunteers.** Enjoy the meal together and ask participants to raise a glass to volunteers' efforts. Encourage sharing of positive, volunteer-related memories from the year.

3. **Host a secret gift exchange.** Set a price range, then recruit willing staff or board members, matching each with one volunteer and directions to provide secret accolades and small gifts. Offer volunteer-specific suggestions, such as a gas gift card for the volunteer who drives 30 miles one-way to help your cause, or a basket of gift tags and bags for the volunteer expecting a household of grandchildren for the holidays.

4. **Conduct a gratitude roundtable.** This could be a simple gathering of volunteers, volunteer managers, select clients and staff to discuss the year's accomplishments, recognize major volunteer achievements and develop efforts for the coming year.

Volunteer Recognition Idea

Have you ever considered using your organization's board meetings to recognize key volunteers' special contributions?

Make a point to invite deserving volunteers to be introduced at each meeting. Doing so provides a special kind of recognition and also emphasizes volunteers' contributions among board members.

RECOGNITION AND APPRECIATION MEASURES

Honor Volunteers by Donating in Their Names

Consider offering a monetary award to add a philanthropic touch to your next volunteer awards ceremony.

Whatcom Volunteer Center (Bellingham, WA) has celebrated volunteers in Whatcom County through its Heart & Hands Award since 2000. The center works to match volunteers with 350 nonprofits, schools, government agencies and healthcare organizations serving the region.

To earn the Heart & Hands Award presented at the Celebration of Service event each April, volunteers are nominated by colleagues, fellow volunteers and community members.

In 2010, the center received 54 nominations and, of those, three jurors selected five volunteers as final candidates. All five honorees received a certificate of appreciation, engraved vase and recognition in front of 250 guests at the volunteer appreciation event. Recipients also received written acknowledgement at the center's website detailing their outstanding service.

Each volunteer also received a special philanthropic gift, says Sue Ellen Heflin, executive director. "The selected award winners received a donation made in their name to the nonprofit of their choice," says Heflin. "This year, five awards of $200 each were given to nonprofits of the award recipient's choosing."

Source: Sue Ellen Heflin, Executive Director, Whatcom Volunteer Center, Bellingham, WA. Phone (360) 734-3055. E-mail: SueEllenH@whatcomvolunteer.org. Website: www.whatcomvolunteer.org

---

Six Groups to Ask to Serve as Volunteer Award Selection Jurors

Each year, exemplary volunteers at the Whatcom Volunteer Center (Bellingham, WA) are honored with its Heart & Hands Award. The process requires jurors to sift through the award nominations and select the final candidates.

If you are looking for candidates to review and select recipients of an award at your volunteer ceremony, consider asking a sampling of representatives from this list to act as your award jurors:

1. Volunteers and volunteer leaders within your community.
2. Newspaper staffers from your regional or hometown newspaper.
3. Event sponsors.
4. Professors or staff from the local university or community college.
5. Retired senior professionals.
6. Community leaders.

Ways to Recognize the Efforts of Long-distance Volunteers

Although it's just as important to recognize the efforts of volunteers assisting you from far-off locations, it can sometimes be more challenging to identify easy ways of doing so.

Make time to create a menu of recognition strategies for these more distant ambassadors. Examples may include:

- A lapel pin or piece of jewelry that designates their relationship to your agency.
- Scheduled phone calls (to discuss business) and unscheduled calls (to pat them on the back).
- Insider news sent regularly to let them know they're special.
- Phone calls from higher ups (board members, the CEO,

and others) thanking them.

- Publishing their names as "VIVs" (very important volunteers).
- Placing an ad in their local newspaper to publicly thank them.
- Sending an occasional photo of something special taking place at your facility.
- Mass-producing a video of a special event or ceremony and sending copies.
- Sending a card and personal note at unexpected times.

Initiate Your Volunteer Hall of Fame

When it comes to managing volunteers, Iowa is definitely doing something right.

Four of Iowa's major communities — Des Moines, Cedar Rapids, Iowa City and Waterloo-Cedar Falls — rank among the top 10 cities in volunteerism efforts, according to the 2009 Volunteering in America Report by the Corporation for National and Community Service (Washington, DC). Iowa City boasted a rate of 49 percent of adults engaging in volunteer activity, while Iowa ranked fifth among states for volunteerism overall.

Check out the 2010 report, Volunteering in America, by the Corporation for National Community Service (Washington, D.C.), including individual state rankings, at: www.volunteeringinamerica.gov

With so many Iowans volunteering, it stands to reason that Iowa takes volunteering seriously. In fact, top volunteers are recognized annually by the Iowa Volunteer Hall of Fame.

Created in 1989 by the Governor's Office for Volunteerism to honor Iowans who make extraordinary donations of volunteer service to their communities, the program is now administered by the Iowa Commission on Volunteer Service (ICVS), Des Moines, IA.

"Being inducted into the Iowa Volunteer Hall of Fame is the most prestigious state-level honor volunteers can receive (and) is truly a once-in-a-lifetime honor, since previous inductees may not be nominated again," says Jody Benz, ICVS volunteer promotion and events coordinator. "The people selected are those who have forever changed their community, the state, the nation or the world with their volunteer service and action."

Fellow Iowans can nominate exceptional volunteers in one of these categories:

- Individual • Organization/Nonprofit
- Group • Family
- Labor Union • Business/Corporation

A ceremony in the Iowa State Capitol during the commission-sponsored annual Volunteer Awareness Day recognizes inductees, whose names are engraved on the Iowa Volunteer Hall of Fame plaque on permanent display in the Iowa Historical Building.

Source: Jody Benz, Volunteer Promotion and Events Coordinator, Iowa Commission on Volunteer Service, Des Moines, IA. Phone: (515) 725-3094. E-mail: jody.benz@iowalifechanging.com

---

Follow Iowa's Example to Honor Volunteers

Following Iowa's nomination criteria and eligibility standards, follow these steps to initiate a Volunteer Hall of Fame in your state — or within your organization:

❑ *Appoint a staff person to coordinate the program.* This person must be able to devote time needed, especially during the nomination/selection cycle.

❑ *Form a committee to work with the coordinator to establish a budget, timeline, nomination criteria and select honorees.* The Iowa Commission on Volunteer Service's promotion, advocacy and recognition committee makes selection recommendations, which go to the governor's office for final approval.

❑ *Promote, promote, promote!* Seek nominees via press releases, newsletters and e-mail messages. Have staff and committee members share information in their own networks. Promote the program on your website and all ways possible to ensure quality nominations are received.

Motivating Volunteers: 109 Techniques to Maximize Volunteer Involvement & Productivity

REGULAR AND VARIED COMMUNICATION IS CRITICAL

Well-conceived communications are critical to the success of any volunteer program. But where volunteer communications used to end with letters, notes and plaques, volunteer managers today must navigate the less familiar waters of tweeting and texting, blogging and friending. The following articles offer a wealth of ideas for clearly conveying information and emotion to volunteers, regardless of the medium used.

Use All Options Available to Communicate With Volunteers

Volunteers lead full lives and have many demands on their time. Communicating with them effectively will ensure that your volunteer events are well-managed and that volunteers receive all necessary information to stay on top of their assignments.

Use the following communications tools to reach your volunteers:

1. **Facebook** — Ask current and incoming volunteers to become fans of your organization's Facebook page so they can receive Facebook posts about upcoming volunteer opportunities at your nonprofit.

2. **Website** — Create an event-specific volunteer page at your organization's website where volunteers can get details about your cause, sign up for specific volunteer tasks and garner information about the event.

3. **E-mail blasts** — Use e-mail as your primary communication tool during event planning. Make messages detailed and specific. E-mail announcements to all volunteers involved in the event, to assign specific roles to each volunteer and to keep them posted about changes. Don't forget to add the critical information as to when the volunteers should arrive, what attire they should be wearing and any items they will need to bring with them.

4. **Text** — Use text messaging to inform volunteers of updates the day of the event. Be sure to get cell numbers in advance of the event so they are stored in your cell in case notifications need to be sent out. Ask volunteers to contact you by cell phone the day of the event to avoid any errant messages that you won't get by e-mail or office voicemail.

5. **Event newsletter** — Create an event-specific newsletter as a wrap-up to all events that involved volunteers. Use it to inform your volunteers about the success of the event, to send kudos to your high-achieving volunteers and to offer thanks for their individual efforts. Include photos of the volunteers in action, and on the last page, create a thank-you page. On the thank-you page, list all volunteers who participated in the event. Check this list carefully so no name is misspelled and no volunteer is omitted.

Give Volunteers, Newcomers a Reason to Volunteer

With people busier than ever now, your job as a volunteer manager is to give them a clear, compelling reason to volunteer.

Every communication you send or post for current and potential volunteers should include at least three ways that volunteering benefits the volunteers. Consider these:

1. **Volunteering is good for your health!** It's a proven fact, volunteering is good for you, emotionally and physically. According to the Corporation for National & Community Service, volunteering has a positive effect on physical and mental health, volunteering lowers the rate of depression among those 65 and older and volunteering increases levels of self-worth.

2. **Volunteering will bond your family!** Volunteering can be done as a family, and the family that volunteers together, stays together.

3. **Volunteering offers many unexpected benefits!** List in detail the benefits volunteers receive at your organization. Do they get a free lunch the day they volunteer? Free health checks? Free admission to your annual gala? Gift shop discounts? The chance to learn new skills or share their knowledge with others? Tell them!

Set Aside Correspondence Time

There's nothing more personal and appreciated than a handwritten letter or note — especially in this day of e-mails, texts and tweets.

When someone goes out of his/her way to write and bring one up to date on important and not-so-important matters, or to say thank-you for a job well done, it is meaningful and appreciated.

Make a point to write personal notes and letters to volunteers regularly. Set aside one day each month to write birthday cards, notes recognizing their volunteering birthday, as well as just-because notes. Share insider information, let them know you're aware of what they are contributing, and leave them with a lasting memory of why their assistance means so much.

REGULAR AND VARIED COMMUNICATION IS CRITICAL

Confirm Volunteer Assignments in Writing

What tools do you provide your volunteers to help them succeed?

As you work with multiple numbers of volunteers on projects requiring their individualized follow-up, your odds of having them complete assigned tasks will improve significantly if you provide each volunteer with written confirmation of what it is he/she is supposed to do (and by when).

Whenever you conduct a meeting in which volunteers leave with agreed-to tasks, immediately send them a personalized memo — as opposed to a standardized group memo — confirming their duties. Spell out exactly what is expected of them, and be sure to include a deadline for the project (or multiple deadlines for portions of the project).

In addition to delineating each task, clearly state how to report back or turn in completed work. This helps bring closure to the task.

Here are two techniques you may want to include in your memo:

1. Offer an incentive for completing tasks on time.

2. Add a final sentence to your memo indicating that all persons not having completed their tasks by the stated deadline will be contacted by you (or the appropriate person) to determine what needs to happen in order to finish the project. Adding a closing statement such as this motivates volunteers to avoid the embarrassment of being contacted, while at the same time, provides you with a justifiable reason for following up with them.

Example of a memo confirming a volunteer's duties:

December 3, 2010   St. Joseph's Hospital
FOUNDATION

TO: Tom Peterson, Sponsorship Committee
FROM: Brenda M. Hawley, Sponsorship Chairperson
RE: Calls to Be Completed By February 15
CC: Debra M. Brown, Director of Alumni

Thank you, Tom, for attending the November 13 Sponsorship Committee meeting and agreeing to call on the following businesses to serve as sponsors for our upcoming event.

As you know, it's imperative that we have commitments from these businesses by February 15 if we are to remain on schedule with our event timeline. For that reason, I am suggesting you schedule appointments for this week and next so business owners and managers have sufficient time to make a decision.

Please turn in (or fax) your completed calls to the Office of Alumni as you complete them. The fax number is 465-9097. As was mentioned at our meeting, those who turn in all calls on time will receive two 50 percent off coupons for dinner at Winchester's.

I encourage you to call me or Debra Brown if you have any questions, need any assistance or experience any difficulty that would impede your ability to complete these calls on schedule.

I will plan to contact any persons who have not turned in their calls to the Office of Alumni by February 15.

Thank you for your valuable assistance with this portion of our 2011 Celebrity Speaker Event.

Sponsorship Calls to be Completed by Tom Peterson by February 15:

- Benders Office Supply & Equipment
- Determan Pepsi Distributors
- Osborne Trucking, Inc.
- Klein Brokers
- Castrole Travel
- Peterson Photography
- MasterCuts
- Winston Raceway

Volunteer Management Blogs Offer Tips, Resources

Blogs have become a mainstream way for volunteers and volunteer managers to share insights and stay informed and connected within the nonprofit community.

Offering interactive opportunities to connect and share online, blogs can offer useful tips, information and resources to volunteer managers.

Search online for blogs that offer information pertinent to your nonprofit or about volunteer management techniques. Check out these to get you started:

- **Engaging Volunteers** — Found at the VolunteerMatch website, this blog offers expert advice and experiences in the volunteering community.

- **IdealistNews** — This free service for nonprofits from Idealist.org and Reddit.com offers insights and information about volunteer management and new trends in the workplace.

- **New York Nonprofit Press** — This blog by Volunteer Administration Practitioner Alexandra Collier offers information in the field of volunteer management, new program ideas and perspectives.

REGULAR AND VARIED COMMUNICATION IS CRITICAL

Volunteer Blog Promotes Communication

Create a volunteer blog exclusively available to your volunteer management team and your steadfast volunteers to streamline communication within your nonprofit. Consider these benefits of hosting a volunteer blog at your organization's website:

- Volunteer managers can communicate with all volunteers at one time regarding upcoming events, changes to policy, volunteer openings and much more.
- Volunteers have unlimited access to updates within your nonprofit that directly involve them.
- Volunteer coordinators can post volunteer schedules for easy access.
- Volunteers can post status updates regarding their role in an upcoming event.
- Photos of volunteer activities can be easily uploaded to the site.
- Volunteers can recruit additional volunteers by talking up the blog to friends, family and colleagues.

Free Sites to Host Your Blog

Use one of these blog hosting sites to start your free volunteer blog today:

✓ www.blogger.com

✓ www.wordpress.com

✓ www.weebly.com

- Event updates, changes or cancellations can be posted immediately to keep all volunteers informed up to and through the day of an event.
- Volunteer activity feedback, kudos and event success details can be added, bringing extra value to your volunteerism activities.
- And finally, a blog can be an archive of your volunteerism activities. Have volunteer coordinators and volunteers post their how-to for creating a particular event and provide feedback for future positive changes to the event.

Boost Volunteer Contact By Tweeting With Twitter

For many nonprofit organizations, social networking is the new norm when communicating with volunteers and staff.

Twitter offers a new way to communicate with a number of individuals simultaneously using instant messaging via text messaging or online. In lieu of sending multiple messages to a variety of individuals, Twitter lets you reach a number of people with a single message.

Individual Twitter messages are referred to as tweets.

While Twitter allows you to send messages to many individuals at one time, it also allows you to gain feedback from this same group.

Use Twitter within your nonprofit to:

- Allow volunteers to view a window on your day.
- Take immediate polls from staff or volunteers to aid in decision making or implementing new ideas.
- Organize instant meetings called "Tweetups."
- Send positive messages about your nonprofit to a select group of volunteers.
- Send instant information to volunteers about changes in scheduling or new happenings at your nonprofit.
- Request that existing volunteers recruit a friend to volunteer.

Consider the Merits of a Volunteer Insiders' Newsletter

If you already have or would like to build a large corps of volunteers, it may be wise to develop a monthly or quarterly newsletter just for them. In addition to spoon-feeding information that can be useful for both existing and potential volunteers, you will also be creating an additional volunteer benefit by offering the newsletter.

Here are some examples of the kinds of information that can be included:

- Regular listings of new volunteers assisting your organization.
- Annual listings of volunteers celebrating anniversaries

with your organization.

- Insider news of the organization that has not yet been released to the media.
- Announcements of new projects that require volunteer involvement.
- Profiles of completed projects that involved volunteers with their names listed.
- Profiles of individual volunteers who have set an example for others to follow.
- Training information that will help volunteers improve their performance.

REGULAR AND VARIED COMMUNICATION IS CRITICAL

Make Time to Walk the Walk

Do you have volunteers who regularly perform tasks efficiently with little or no staff involvement? If so, work by their side for a shift or two.

By walking in their shoes, you will better understand their work experience and discover ways to make their work more rewarding for them. Be observant of things such as:

- **Work environment** — proper lighting, noise level, adequate space, comfort and other physical aspects that may need to be changed.

- **Work process** — who does what when, steps that may be unnecessary, ideas that may make their work operate more efficiently and effectively and more.

- **Work mood** — camaraderie, personality conflicts, competition and job satisfaction.

Taking time to be part of the volunteers' work experience will help you see tasks from volunteers' perspectives while also sending them the message that you appreciate their efforts and are willing to walk alongside of them to get the job done.

Encourage On-site Visits for Virtual Volunteers

Strengthen relationships with your virtual volunteers by encouraging onsite visits.

Doing so is especially important when a volunteer is beginning work with your nonprofit. An in-person meeting will give the volunteer a chance to talk with you face-to-face and feel more connected to your organization and its mission.

When an onsite visit isn't possible, a phone call is the next best way to maintain your relationship with these increasingly valuable volunteers.

Relationship-building Tip

- It's been said that when you start relationship building and then stop, it's worse than not having started at all. Know that each new introduction requires ongoing attention and nurturing.

Keep Helpful Volunteers in the Information Loop

Just as it's important to demonstrate good stewardship to financial contributors, it's equally important to show sound stewardship practices to volunteers who make inroads on your behalf.

Take this East Coast college for example: One of the institution's graduates volunteered to introduce a major gift prospect to college officials and played a key role in what resulted in a $200,000 scholarship gift. The volunteer was surprised to learn several months later that college officials had reapproached the donor for more funding without even informing the helpful volunteer of their plans. As it turned out, the donor gave a paltry second gift and the volunteer felt betrayed having been left out of the loop.

Whenever you are fortunate enough to have a volunteer who has made inroads on your behalf — introduced you to a new donor or recruited a new corporate volunteer to assist

your effort — remember to keep that volunteer fully informed long after he/she has completed the upfront work:

1. If and when you plan to take further action with a volunteer-introduced individual or idea, at the very least, inform him/her of your plans.

2. Seek the input of the volunteer before taking further action.

3. Copy any correspondence to the helpful volunteer as a way to keep him/her in the loop.

Although you may be fully capable of carrying the baton on your own, the volunteer who was initially involved will feel a much greater sense of accomplishment and contribution if he/she is made aware of activities happening subsequent to his/her initial work.

REGULAR AND VARIED COMMUNICATION IS CRITICAL

Personalize Post-event Volunteer Notes of Thanks

When wrapping up a fundraising event, don't forget one important detail — tell your volunteers "thank you!"

The Food Bank for Larimer County (Fort Collins, CO) hosts four signature fundraisers each year, each requiring the assistance of approximately 100 volunteers. Once an event wraps, volunteers receive a personalized thank-you note with specific details about how their contribution truly made a difference.

Charlene Olms, volunteer and development coordinator, sends a letter to each volunteer after every event stating how much was raised in total and how much the silent auction raised, including a personalized note specific to that event.

Olms says organizers of one of this year's fundraisers met with an unusual challenge when several volunteers fell ill and others had to pick up the slack. Olms was sure to mention this in her thank-you note and recognized those who stepped in to cover with a gift certificate for an ice cream treat.

Olms also includes her e-mail address in the thank-you note asking the volunteers to contact her with their ideas and suggestions for event success in the future.

When sending a personalized thank-you note, follow these tips:

- Handwrite the note whenever possible for an extra personal touch.

- Note the significant contributions volunteers made at the fundraiser. Be specific. Detail amount raised at the event (or other goals achieved) and note how much was raised from each component of the night, especially where volunteers were involved, such as the silent auction.

- Mention the special ways in which volunteers went above and beyond the call of duty specific to the event.

- Add a small gift of thanks such as a gift certificate as a token of your appreciation.

- Include your contact information in the note so volunteers can reach you with their comments and/or suggestions about the event.

Source: Charlene Olms, Volunteer and Development Coordinator, Food Bank for Larimer County, Fort Collins, CO. Phone (970) 530-3113. E-mail: colms@foodbanklarimer.org

Motivating Volunteers: 109 Techniques to Maximize Volunteer Involvement & Productivity

HOW OTHERS ARE ENERGIZING VOLUNTEERS

The example of others, their successes and failures, can be a powerful source of ideas and learning. To see how other nonprofits are making the most of their volunteering program — whether in motivation, training, productivity, satisfaction, communication or recognition — consider the winning ideas and proven initiatives in the following profiles.

Website Photo Gallery Shows Volunteers in Action

I Love a Clean San Diego (ILACSD) of San Diego, CA, is a nonprofit whose staff and supporters perform community outreach and actively conserve and enhance the environment. Committing to these goals requires the help of more than 25,000 volunteers a year.

The ILACSD website contains a photo gallery featuring snapshots of volunteer projects including cleanup days at rivers, lakes and oceanfronts. Clicking on a project header, the viewer is taken to another window showing all of the photos associated with that specific project individually or via a slideshow.

"We take photos at each event to capture the impact made by volunteers and by our organization," says Natalie Roberts, director of community events. "This is a powerful tool to show before and after shots, encourage volunteerism, and show individuals the impact they can have on their community by getting involved. Photos also are an important educational tool to show others how their behaviors compile and affect environments to encourage eco-friendly daily habits that conserve our environment."

Photos posted at the ILACSD website are taken and managed by staff members to ensure that only approved photos are represented. If your organization wants to begin or improve the volunteer photos used on your website, follow these tips:

✓ Capture many candid and posed photos in the midst of each event or project involving volunteers.

✓ Take photos of site visits in advance of volunteers arriving to show the dramatic accomplishments made by volunteers who are removing litter or debris.

✓ Also be sure to capture after photos to show how the project site has changed with the efforts of the volunteers.

✓ Select the most active and artfully composed shots to post on the website. Avoid using all photos just for the sake of using them. Volunteer photos need to be dynamic to draw the attention of new volunteers!

Source: Natalie Roberts, Director of Community Events, I Love a Clean San Diego, San Diego, CA. Phone (619) 291-0103. E-mail: nroberts@cleansd.org. Website: www.cleansd.org

A Basket Full of Thanks Honors Volunteers

A volunteer manager with limited funds decided to ask recipients of volunteer service for help with Volunteer Week recognition. She invited department leaders to participate by filling an appreciation basket with personal notes or small gifts.

During a monthly staff meeting, the volunteer manager explained the purpose of the basket. She handed out a sample message, a list of volunteer names, a list of gift suggestions and designer note paper.

During the next week, items could be deposited in the basket in her office. At the end of the week, the basket contained:

- Personal thank you notes to specific volunteers.
- Copies of an original cartoon created by the CEO.
- Signed appreciation letters from department leaders.
- Car wash certificates for all volunteers.
- A box of chocolates for each person.

- A poster-sized thank-you card. Employees wrote a personal note under their photo.
- A box of nuts for the volunteer office.
- A T-shirt and cap for each volunteer.
- Purse-size lotion for each volunteer.
- Three dozen roses.
- Windshield shades, movie tickets, mall certificates, duffle bags, first-aid kits and flashlights. These gifts included instructions to present the gift to volunteers who worked the most hours, the one who traveled the farthest, the oldest/youngest, etc.

During a Volunteer Week luncheon, the appreciation basket was presented to volunteers, who were overwhelmed with the recognition.

Clean, Precise Volunteering Web Page Serves Hospital Well

The website for George Washington University Hospital (Washington, D.C.) offers volunteers a clean and precise volunteering page.

Visitors to the main page of the volunteering section find easy step-by-step instructions on becoming volunteers and are just a click away from finding volunteer opportunities at the hospital.

In the past year, Kristin Urbach, director of customer and volunteer service, has recruited 366 volunteers who have provided 16,000 hours of service. Urbach says the volunteering page served as a starting point for many of those volunteers, guiding them through the volunteering process.

Every month, nearly 1,600 Web searchers access the volunteer page at GWU, she says. Here, Urbach tells us more about this high-traffic online volunteer resource:

How does the clean appearance of your volunteering Web page benefit would-be volunteers?

"Due to the information and appearance on our website, in addition to changing the application process to an online one, we have been able to recruit more candidates."

When volunteers call in inquiring about opportunities, are they simply directed to the Volunteer page since the steps are outlined so cleanly?

"When volunteers call about opportunities, we respond to their questions and also provide them with the website address. When they call us, we want to be able to provide great customer service by thanking them for their interest, responding to their questions and directing them to the website. When they do not reach a live person, the voicemail provides our website address and recommends they review it for information. As a result, we do not receive many calls because the website is informative and user-friendly."

Source: Kristin Urbach, Director of Customer and Volunteer Service, George Washington University Hospital, Washington, D.C. Phone (202) 715-4188. E-mail: Kristin.urbach@gwu-hospital.com. Website: www.gwhospital.com

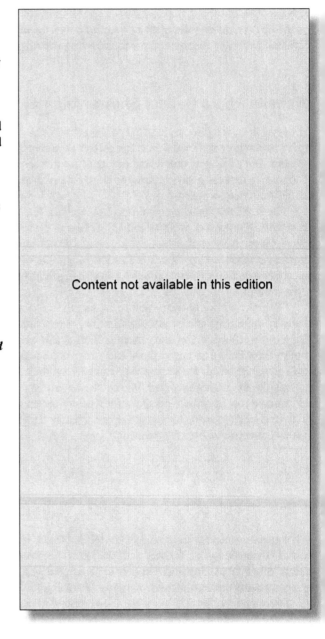

Content not available in this edition

Labels Draw Awareness to Volunteer Efforts

Consider labeling your volunteer-assembled items and volunteer-created projects to draw attention to their efforts within your organization.

Volunteers at LifeCare Medical Center (Roseau, MN) fulfill a great array of volunteer tasks. Whether assembling information folders, admission packets, pamphlets or filling plastic eggs for the annual Easter egg hunt, they place a sticker on the item that reads: "Assembled by the caring hands of our Volunteers at LifeCare Medical Center."

"These labels trigger the minds of those utilizing the information that a volunteer's hands created that item," says Pam Sando, volunteer coordinator, "drawing awareness to our volunteer efforts and also putting our name on each item."

Source: Pam Sando and Terry Lamppa, Volunteer Coordinators, LifeCare Medical Center, Roseau, MN. Phone (218) 463-4714. E-mail: Volunteer@lifecaremc.com

Tips to Keep Volunteers Coming Back for Ongoing Events

Second Harvest North Florida (Jacksonville, FL) has put on an Empty Bowls event for 25 years, most recently raising $75,000 to help end hunger in Florida.

With the assistance of 50 volunteers, the event has become a seamless process, says Tia Ford, advancement coordinator-special events.

Here, Ford offers her best tips for volunteer management:

❑ Match volunteers with tasks and responsibilities they will enjoy, keeping their interests in mind. This way, they will enjoy what they are doing, be more likely to volunteer again and have a sense of accomplishment for the positive impact they are making on the organization.

❑ Diversify your volunteer corps. Don't keep going back to the same group of volunteers for every volunteer need, or you risk becoming dependent on them. They could end up holding significant knowledge about your event, project or program. And when they get burned out, they take that knowledge with them.

❑ Define expectations with your volunteers up front. Share what you hope they can bring to your event or program, and find out what they would like to gain from helping your event/program — whether it's simply community service hours, the opportunity to learn more about your organization, help an organization that once helped them, networking or other motivating factor.

Source: Tia Ford, Advancement Coordinator-Special Events, Second Harvest North Florida, Jacksonville, FL. Phone (904) 730-8284. E-mail: TFord@lssjax.org

Advice to Keep Youth Volunteers Motivated

High school and college-age students are invaluable to the volunteer workforce at Deaconess Medical Center and Valley Hospital and Medical Center (Spokane, WA).

Each student session, employees welcome a new group of student volunteers to help with healthcare tasks and shadow them on the job. Students are allowed access to emergency rooms and, in a highly supervised way, operating viewing rooms.

Joey Frost, director of volunteer services, offers advice regarding specific elements when working with volunteers ages 14-22:

❑ **Applicant interview and evaluation** — When you interview youth volunteers, discuss specifics about their commitment level and schedules to determine if they are already too overcommitted with activities and school to make time for volunteer efforts. Frost notes that some applicants apply only to appease wishes of parents or a college application board.

❑ **References** — As with any other position, have students apply for volunteer roles. Call on references to learn the student's level of maturity and responsibility before assigning a specific position. At the medical center where Frost supervises volunteers, staff help determine applicants' ability to handle emergency situations.

❑ **Flexibility** — Student volunteers need flexibility in their schedules to accommodate course work. By creating a flexible scheduling plan, Deaconess and Valley garnered a more dedicated volunteer base. During quiet times, information and guest relations desk volunteers are allowed to study while on duty, allowing them necessary study time while fulfilling a useful role.

❑ **Variety** — Responsibility and variety help young people stay excited about volunteering. Frost allows students to move into various areas of the healthcare system each semester to give them a varied exposure and keep them engaged.

❑ **Boundaries** — Be clear as to the rules of your organization. With cell phone and iPod usage skyrocketing among teens, Frost makes it clear that these devices are not allowed during volunteer shifts.

❑ **Policy review** — Provide volunteers and their parents with a copy of the procedure manual for your institution. Have both the volunteer and parents sign a form stating they've carefully read the manual to prevent future misunderstandings.

❑ **Program evaluation** — Utilize your current youth volunteers to determine areas of improvement needed in your program. After speaking with high school volunteers who expressed boredom with some volunteer roles, Frost found she could combine two service areas — pharmacy delivery and front desk — to keep volunteers busy and more efficient in their volunteer efforts.

Source: Joey Frost, Director of Volunteer Services, Deaconess Medical Center and Valley Hospital and Medical Center, Spokane, WA. Phone (509) 473-3767. E-mail: FrostJ@Empirehealth.org

Volunteer Management Steps Save Time, Retain Volunteers

Having the right volunteer management tools can help you save valuable time.

Deb Johnson-Schad, program coordinator, Common Good Retired Senior Volunteer Program (Winona, MN), helps support numerous volunteer programs and 220 volunteers age 55 and older.

Johnson-Schad offers the following tips for managing volunteers efficiently:

- Keep your database of volunteer opportunities and volunteers updated. Common Good RSVP uses Volunteer Reporter software offered by Volunteer Software (Missoula, MT), which allows users to enter in volunteer interests and skills as well as those needed by volunteer sites. "We can run reports to match need with volunteers, but in order to be effective," Johnson-Schad says, "we need to keep everything current, especially contact names, e-mail addresses and phone numbers."

- Know your current volunteer station needs. The needs of nonprofits are continually in flux. Keep a current inventory of volunteer needs and open positions. Obtaining a complete job description for each role at the outset and continually updating it will save a lot of time.

- Know your volunteers. Call volunteers regularly to see if their schedules have changed, evaluate when their current schedules allow for volunteering and update their areas of volunteer interests.

- Respond to all e-mails and phone calls within 24 hours. If not, you lose credibility. If you are unavailable for a day or two, update your phone recording and e-mail with this information.

- Follow up. Always follow up with volunteer sites and volunteers to see how things are going. You may be able to resolve any problems or conflict at the outset, which will aid volunteer retention.

Source: Deb Johnson-Schad, Program Coordinator, Common Good RSVP, Northfield, MN. Phone (507) 649-1699. E-mail: dschad@ccwinona.org

Tell Volunteers 'Thanks a Latté!'

When Becca Wexler, volunteer coordinator, Village Shalom, Inc. (Overland Park, KS) wants to thank her volunteers, she says "thanks a latté!"

More than 150 volunteers were invited to a Starbucks coffee tasting organized as a show of appreciation for their service to the retirement community. A Starbucks barista conducted a presentation on coffee types, flavors, aromas and the best food pairings to have with each type of coffee.

Here are a few tips for hosting your own volunteer appreciation coffee tasting:

- Invite a local barista to share expertise on coffees and food pairings.
- Decorate tables with a coffee theme. Wexler used greens, browns and creams as coordinating table colors and sprinkled tables with coffee beans.
- Create invitations with a coffee theme. The Thanks a Latté! invitation had a picture of a steaming cup of coffee on the front. Wexler ordered invitations from VistaPrint, an online source she says offers quality invitations at a reasonable cost.
- Consider time of day. While the Thanks a Latté! event was in the evening, planners have decided it may be more successful held in the morning since guests will be trying caffeinated coffees.

- Encourage volunteer participation with giveaway opportunities. Each volunteer attending the event received a coffee mug, and attendees were entered into a contest to win coffee gift cards and other prizes.

- Use giveaways as part of your decor. Wexler used an earthy and decorative mug, plate and bowl set as centerpieces on the tables and played CDs from the local coffee house that were later used as prizes for guests.

- Purchase items in bulk. Coffee beans for the event came from Sam's Club.

"Thanks a Latté was a fun and creative approach to recognizing our volunteers," says Wexler. "The volunteers were introduced to various Starbucks roasts as they got to know each other over a rich cup of coffee."

Source: Becca Wexler, Volunteer Coordinator, Village Shalom, Inc., Overland Park, KS. Phone (913) 266-8310. E-mail: bwexler@villageshalom.org

HOW OTHERS ARE ENERGIZING VOLUNTEERS

Ideas to Retain Volunteers in a Stress-filled Environment

You invest hours in training your volunteers. Invest equal time in retaining them.

Retention is especially important at CASA at Woodlawn (Danville, KY), where volunteers fulfill the judge-appointed role of advocate for an abused or neglected child who has recently entered the court system.

CASA stands for Court Appointed Special Advocates. To serve in that important role, volunteers undergo 30 hours of intense training to learn to properly assist children facing foster care or new court-appointed living arrangements.

Maureen Draut, volunteer coordinator, shares her ideas on retaining volunteers:

- **Send cards noting special occasions or thinking-of-you cards.** Note important events in the lives of the volunteers to make them feel part of the community and to show their efforts are appreciated.

- **Host simple get-togethers.** Note volunteer efforts by hosting a holiday meal for current and past volunteers. An ice cream social or chili cook-off, where volunteers gather in a relaxed environment, boosts camaraderie and gives volunteers a sense of belonging and appreciation.

- **Communicate by e-mail.** CASA volunteers receive frequent e-mail communications with updates to keep them in the loop and to give them a continued sense of belonging.

- **Offer conferences and continuing education.** When possible, invite volunteers to conferences or trainings to increase their education and skills to and keep them a involved in the organization.

- **Increase staff.** CASA will soon include two new staff positions to assist Draut in managing its volunteer base. While increasing staff is not always a consideration due to budget concerns, you may want to evaluate your organization's staffing needs to ensure that volunteers are getting the necessary staff attention for smooth operations.

Source: Maureen Draut, Volunteer Coordinator, CASA at Woodlawn, Danville, KY. Phone (859) 936-3546. E-mail: Maureen@casaatwoodlawn.org

Support Long-term Volunteers

Here's an idea to celebrate volunteers:

Linda Dean, director of volunteer services, Jackson Hospital (Montgomery, AL), created the Volunteer Emeritus Award to honor five retiring volunteers who served a combined 140 years at the hospital. Through the award, the retiring volunteers and other volunteers of Jackson Hospital serving more than 20 years receive:

- ✓ **An honorary reception:** Complete with refreshments and musical entertainment, the reception features the hospital CEO thanking them for their service plus a plaque presentation.

- ✓ **A special badge:** In exchange for their working volunteer ID badge, retiring volunteers are given a volunteer emeritus ID badge that gives access to volunteer areas and events at the hospital.

- ✓ **Lifetime free lunches** with working volunteers and **free parking** in the coveted, gated volunteer parking area.

"The devotion and loyalty of these volunteers is rare in today's world," says Dean. "I felt honored to have these ladies in my program and to witness firsthand the kind of commitment this generation believes in."

Source: Linda Dean, Director of Volunteer Services, Jackson Hospital, Montgomery, AL. Phone (334) 293-8967. E-mail: DeanL@jackson.org